Jack C. Richards & Chuck Sandy

Passages

Second Edition

D1608683

1

Student's Book

CAMBRIDGE
UNIVERSITY PRESS

CAMBRIDGE UNIVERSITY PRESS
Cambridge, New York, Melbourne, Madrid, Cape Town,
Singapore, São Paulo, Delhi, Mexico City

Cambridge University Press
32 Avenue of the Americas, New York, NY 10013-2473, USA

www.cambridge.org
Information on this title: www.cambridge.org/9780521683869

First published 1998
Second Edition 2008
18th printing 2013

Printed in Hong Kong, China, by Golden Cup Printing Company Limited

A catalog record for this publication is available from the British Library.

Library of Congress Cataloging-in-Publication Data
Richard, Jack C.
 Passages: [an upper-level multi-skills course]: student's book 1 / Jack C. Richards & Chuck Sandy. – 2nd ed.
   p. cm.
 ISBN 978-0-521-68386-9 (pbk. with cd/cd-rom)
 1. English language – Textbooks for foreign speakers. I. Sandy, Chuck. II. Title.

PE1128.R4598 2008
428.2'4–dc22

                              2007036210

ISBN 978-0-521-68386-9 student's book and self-study audio CD / CD-ROM (Windows, Mac)
ISBN 978-0-521-68388-3 workbook
ISBN 978-0-521-68387-6 teacher's edition and audio CD
ISBN 978-0-521-68390-6 CDs (audio)

Art direction, book design, photo research, and layout services: Adventure House, NYC
Audio production: Paul Ruben Productions

Authors' Acknowledgments

A great number of people contributed to the development of *Passages, Second Edition.* Particular thanks are owed to the following:

The **reviewers** using *Passages* in the following schools and institutes – their insights and suggestions have helped define the content and format of the second edition: Maria Elizabeth Andrews from **Proficiency School of English**, São Paulo, Brazil; Vera Lúcia Cardoso Berk from **Talkative Idioms Center**, São Paulo, Brazil; coordinators and teachers from **Phil Young's English School**, Curitiba, Brazil; Janette Carvalhinho de Oliveira, Manoel Sampaio Junior, and Sandlei Moraes de Oliveira from **Centro de Línguas para a Comunidade**, Vitória, Brazil; Juliana Costa da Silva, Soraya Farage Martins, Valdemir Pinto da Silva Jr., and Luciana Ribeiro da Silva from **Alternative Language Learning**, Rio de Janeiro, Brazil; Danielle Sampaio Cordeiro from **Sociedade Brasileira de Cultura Inglesa**, Rio de Janeiro, Brazil; Inara Lúcia Castillo Couto from **CEL-LEP**, São Paulo, Brazil; Mailda Flôres Sales, Maria Helena Medrado, and Sávio Siqueira from **ACBEU**, Salvador, Brazil; Angela Graciela Mendonza dos Santos from **Focus Consultoria Educacional**, Rio de Janeiro, Brazil; Caroline Ciagiwoda and Aguirre Pinto Neto from **Exien English School**, Curitiba, Brazil; Evânia A. Netto and Anderson Lopes Siqueira from **ICBEU**, São José dos Campos, Brazil; Silvia Sapiense from **Speed English Center**, São Paulo, Brazil; Michael Twohey from **York University**, Toronto, Canada; Randa Ibrahim Mady and Magda Laurence from the **Centre for Adult and Continuing Education, the American University of Cairo**, Cairo, Egypt; Jamie Dupuis, Dale Palmer, Kent Suder, and Stephanie Wilson from **GEOS**, Japan; Gregory Hadley from **Niigata University of International and Information Studies**, Niigata, Japan; Brian Quinn from **Kyushu University**, Fukuoka, Japan; David Michael Duke, Christine A. Figueroa, and Thomas Greene from **Kyung Hee University**, Seoul, Korea; Jinyoung Hong, Susan Kelly, Young-Ok Kim, Jennifer Lee, and Scott Miles from **Sogang University**, Seoul, Korea; Christopher N. Payne from **Seoul National University, Language Education Institute**, Seoul, Korea; Julia Samuel from **Sahmyook University English Department**, Seoul, Korea; Juan Alvarez Cháves from **Instituto Technologico Superior de Zapotlanejo**, Jalisco, Mexico; Samuel Bolaños Whangpo, Luis G. Dominguez Arellano, and Diana Jones from **Centro Universitario Angloamericano**, Mexico City, Mexico; A. Ezequiel Guerrero Marín and Lino Martín Lugo Córdova from **Centro de Estudio de Idiomas-UAS**, Los Mochis, Mexico; Olga Hernández Badillo, Leticia Moreno Elizalde, and Fernando Perales Vargas from **Facultad de Contaduría y Administración de la Universidad Juarez del Estado de Durango**, Durango, Mexico; Yuriria Tabakova Hernández from **Universidad Latinoamericana**, Mexico City, Mexico; Lucila Mendoza Reyes from **Universidad Autonoma Metropolitana**, Mexico City, Mexico; Roberto López Rodríguez from **Centro de Auto-Aprendizaje de Inglés, Facultad de Ciencias Físico Matemáticas UANL**, San Nicolas de los Garza, Mexico; Elizabeth Almandoz, Susanna D. de Eguren, and Rocío García Valdez from **Instituto Cultural Peruano Norteamericano (ICPNA)**, Miraflores, Peru; Giuliana B. Astorne Guillén from **CED El Buen Pastor**, Lima, Peru; Cecilia Carmelino from **ICPNA**, La Molina, Peru; César Ccaccya Leiva from **ICPNA**, San Miguel, Peru; Amparo García Peña from **ICPNA**, Cusco, Peru; Elizabeth Llatas Castillo from **Centro Binacional El Cultural**, Trujillo, Peru; Claudia Marín Cabrera from **Universidad Peruana de Ciencias Aplicadas**, Lima, Peru; Silvia Osores and María Isabel Valencia from **Colegio de La Immaculada**, Lima, Peru; Samuel Chen from **Taichung YMCA Language School**, Taichung, Taiwan; Shih-Wen Chen from **National Tsing Hua University Department of Foreign Languages and Literature**, Hsinchu, Taiwan; Han-yi Lin from **Center of Foreign Languages, National Chengchi University**, Taipei, Taiwan; Huei-chih Liu from **Shu-Te University**, Kaohsiung, Taiwan; Julie D. Adler, Beth Kozbial Ernst, and Kelly Wonder from **University of Wisconsin-Eau Claire**, Eau Claire, Wisconsin, USA; Renata Concina, Mary Horosco, Margaret A. Lowry, and Luis Sanchez from **The English Language Institute at Florida International University**, Miami, Florida, USA; Mary Gillman from **Des Moines Area Community College**, Des Moines, Iowa, USA; Leslie Lott from **Embassy CES**, Fort Lauderdale, Florida, USA; Paul Paitchell from **Talk International**, Fort Lauderdale, Florida, USA; Elisa Shore from **City College of San Francisco**, San Francisco, California, USA; Theresa E. Villa from **East Los Angeles Skills Center**, Los Angeles, California, USA; Randi Wilder, Upper Saddle River, New Jersey, USA.

The **editorial** and **production** team: Sue Brioux Aldcorn, Sue Andre Costello, Eleanor K. Barnes, David Bohlke, Mike Boyle, Jeff Chen, Sarah Cole, Inara Lucia Castillo Couto, Leslie DeJesus, Jill Freshney, Rod Gammon, Deborah Goldblatt, Paul Heacock, Louisa Hellegers, Lisa Hutchins, Genevieve Kocienda, Cindy Leaney, Linda LiDestri, Andy London, Paul MacIntyre, Diana Nam, Margareth Perucci, Sandra Pike, Mary Sandre, Tamar Savir, Satoko Shimoyama, Susannah Sodergren, Lori Solbakken, Louisa van Houten, Mary Vaughn, Jennifer Wilkin, Jenny Wilsen, and all the design and production team at Adventure House.

And Cambridge University Press **staff** and **advisors**: Sarah Acosta, Harry Ahn, Yumiko Akeba, Jim Anderson, Mary Louise Baez, Kathleen Corley, Kate Cory-Wright, Maiza Fatureto, Claudia Fiocco, Elizabeth Fuzikava, Cecilia Gómez, Heather Gray, Yuri Hara, Catherine Higham, Peter Holly, Jennifer Kim, Robert Kim, Ken Kingery, Kareen Kjelstrup, Gareth Knight, Nigel McQuitty, João Madureira, Andy Martin, Alejandro Martínez, John Moorcroft, Mark O'Neil, Marcus Paiva, Orelly Palmas, Jinhee Park, Walter Quiroz, Carlos Ramírez, Ricardo Romero, Tereza Sekiya, Catherine Shih, Howard Siegelman, Ivan Sorrentino, Ian Sutherland, Alcione Soares Tavares, Koen Van Landeghem, Sergio Varela, and Ellen Zlotnick.

Additional thanks are owed to Cindy Leaney for writing the Self-study section and to Sue Brioux Aldcorn for writing the Grammar Plus section.

Welcome to *Passages!*

Passages, Second Edition, is a two-level course that will help you raise your English to the next level. You've already learned the basics and have progressed to the high-intermediate level. To take you further, *Passages, Second Edition,* emphasizes new and sophisticated grammar and vocabulary, listening and reading texts on more challenging topics, academic writing activities, and thought-provoking discussions.

There is a Self-study section to help build your academic skills, and this book also includes the *Cambridge Academic Content Dictionary* on CD-ROM.

Each unit consists of two four-page lessons. Each lesson contains a variety of exercises, including starting point, vocabulary, grammar, listening, discussion, writing, and reading. Here is a sample unit.

Unit features

Starting point presents new grammar in both formal and conversational contexts.

Grammar activities help you use the new grammar to talk about yourself.

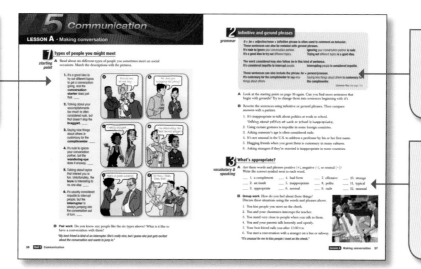

Vocabulary teaches phrasal verbs, prefixes and suffixes, and collocations (words that go together).

Speaking activities include discussions, surveys, personality quizzes, role plays, and more.

Writing builds academic writing skills step by step and gives clear examples for each task.

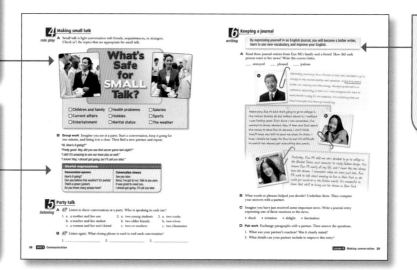

Useful expressions boxes help you manage conversations. For example, this lesson teaches ways to start and end a small-talk conversation.

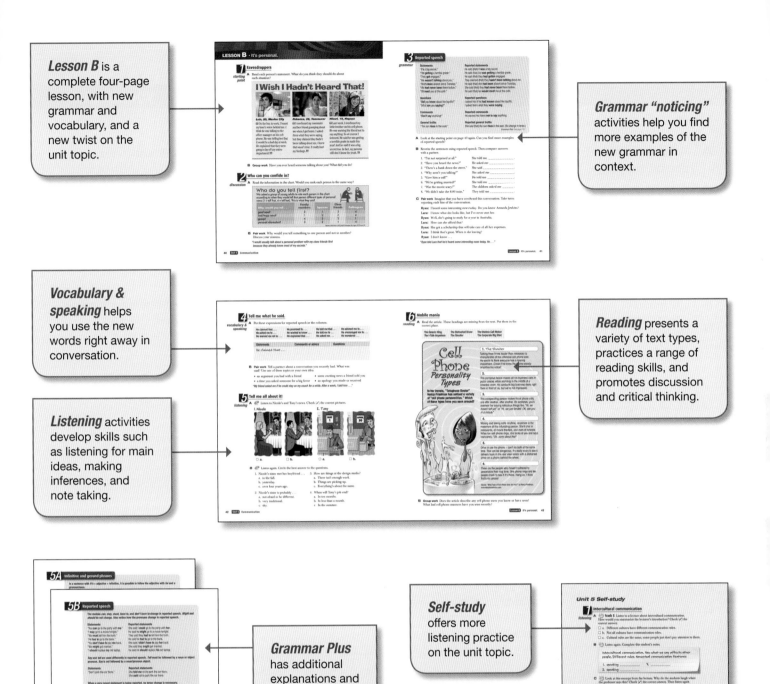

Lesson B is a complete four-page lesson, with new grammar and vocabulary, and a new twist on the unit topic.

Grammar "noticing" activities help you find more examples of the new grammar in context.

Vocabulary & speaking helps you use the new words right away in conversation.

Reading presents a variety of text types, practices a range of reading skills, and promotes discussion and critical thinking.

Listening activities develop skills such as listening for main ideas, making inferences, and note taking.

Grammar Plus has additional explanations and extra practice for each lesson's grammar.

Self-study offers more listening practice on the unit topic.

Dictionary skills activities use the dictionary CD-ROM included in your Student's Book.

More resources

Communication reviews after every three units include progress checks and additional listening and speaking activities.

The **Workbook** gives you language practice and extra reading and writing activities.

The **Teacher's Edition** includes additional games, projects, and readings, as well as written and oral quizzes.

Plan of Book 1

SPEAKING	LISTENING	WRITING	READING
• Finding out what personality traits you have in common with your classmates • Comparing personality profiles • Talking about how you have changed or how you would like to change • Comparing families • Talking about rules and habits in your family	• Two people describe how they have changed • Two people compare similarities and differences between their families • A young man describes his recent family reunion	• Identifying the main idea in a paragraph • Writing a paragraph about your most positive or negative quality	• "Full House: Meet the Silcocks": A family with more than 30 adopted sons
• Talking about your past mistakes • Comparing reactions to a news story • Discussing what might have caused three mysterious events • Making guesses about unusual questions • Comparing opinions about a real-life unexplained event	• A man talks about a bad decision he made • Three people talk about how they dealt with their problems • A radio program discusses a real-life unexplained event	• Brainstorming topic sentences and supporting ideas • Writing a paragraph with dos and don'ts	• "Amnesia Spoils Newlyweds' Bliss": A man loses all his memories during his honeymoon
• Explaining why you'd like to visit a particular city • Choosing the right city for a particular purpose • Deciding which city is best to live in • Describing your hometown • Discussing quality-of-life issues	• A TV show introduces two exciting cities • Two foreign students explain what they like about their host city • Two Sydney residents talk about the city	• Organizing ideas with a mind map • Writing a paragraph about a place you know	• "A Tale of Two Cities": The rivalry between two major Australian cities
• Discussing personal energy levels • Talking about how to deal with stress • Giving advice on sleep and energy levels • Talking about sleeping habits • Interpreting dreams	• Three people describe methods they use to lower stress • Two people describe their dreams and try to interpret them	• Choosing the best topic sentence • Writing a paragraph giving advice on good habits	• "To Sleep or Not to Sleep?": How technology is changing our sleep habits
• Discussing conversational styles • Discussing awkward social situations • Determining appropriate topics for small talk • Comparing who you confide in • Recounting an interesting conversation	• Several people make small talk at a party • Two people tell some interesting news	• Keeping a journal • Writing your reaction to a piece of important news	• "Cell Phone Personality Types": What kind of cell phone user are you?
• Determining if a story is true or false • Presenting a recent news story • Discussing how you follow the news • Telling stories about uncomfortable situations • Creating a story with your classmates	• A radio news broadcast • Two people describe personal dilemmas • An actor describes his most embarrassing moments	• Putting events in order • Writing a narrative paragraph	• "It happened to me!": Two comical personal anecdotes

viii

SPEAKING	LISTENING	WRITING	READING
• Talking about how Internet trends affect you • Debating whether the Internet is a positive or negative influence • Giving opinions on modern information technology • Discussing unusual gadgets	• Three people talk about how they use the Internet • A news report describes health problems caused by technology	• Writing a blog post	• "Can you spare a dime for my Gucci bills?": A woman uses the Internet to get money to pay off a frivolous debt
• Describing jobs that require creativity • Taking a creativity quiz • Suggesting new uses for everyday items • Talking about creative thinking habits • Choosing the inventions that have had the greatest impact on modern life • Explaining why new products are invented	• Three employees explain how their jobs are creative • Two descriptions of important business and product ideas	• Choosing when to begin a new paragraph • Writing a composition about a creative or unique person	• "The Man Who Taught the World to Sing": A profile of the man who invented karaoke
• Talking about what's average • Discussing what makes you typical or unique • Discussing the effect of major life changes • Giving advice in a role play	• Three people discuss how they're unique • Three people describe problems they solved	• Identifying supporting statements • Developing a paragraph with supporting statements	• "Are We Advice Junkies?": How to give effective advice to friends
• Discussing how to handle irritating situations • Comparing styles of complaining • Role-playing complaints • Stating consumer complaints • Describing how difficult situations make you feel	• Two people describe irritating situations • A man uses an automated phone menu	• Writing a letter of complaint	• "Wedding Shop Leaves Brides Waiting at Altar": Two brides deal with a bad consumer experience
• Taking a survey on scruples • Comparing what you would do about different ethical dilemmas • Discussing your experiences with unreliable people or services • Talking about values that are important to you • Explaining what you would choose if you were given three wishes	• Two people describe being confronted by an ethical dilemma • Three people talk about the values that are most important to them	• Writing a thesis statement • Writing a four-paragraph composition about a happy memory or a regret	• "New York Honors a Hero": A profile of Wesley Autrey, subway hero
• Describing the benefits and challenges of living abroad • Comparing customs between North America and your country • Sharing bad travel experiences • Planning a trip with your group	• Three young people talk about their experiences living abroad • Two people describe travel mishaps	• Writing conclusions • Writing a composition about living or traveling abroad	• "Get Yourself Lost": The best way to experience a foreign destination

1 Friends and family

1 Personality survey

starting point

A Do you agree with these statements? Complete the survey.

Personality Survey	Definitely agree	Somewhat agree	Definitely disagree
1. I'm not afraid of giving speeches in front of the class.	○	○	○
2. I enjoy going to parties where I don't know everyone.	○	○	○
3. I avoid expressing my feelings and ideas in public.	○	○	○
4. I insist on making my own decisions.	○	○	○
5. I don't mind giving up my time to help other people.	○	○	○
6. I never worry about getting places on time.	○	○	○
7. I always feel like going dancing!	○	○	○
8. I can't stand being in a messy, disorganized room.	○	○	○
9. I prefer telling people how I feel, even if it's embarrassing.	○	○	○

B **Pair work** Compare your responses to the survey. Find two ways you and your partner are different.

"I'm not afraid of giving speeches in front of the class. How about you?"

"Oh, I'm definitely afraid of doing that!"

2 How would you describe yourself?

vocabulary & speaking

A Which statement from the survey above best matches these personality traits? Write the correct number. Then compare answers with a partner.

_2_ a. friendly and outgoing   ___ d. kind and generous   ___ g. wild and crazy

___ b. strong and independent   ___ e. honest and sincere   ___ h. calm and cool

___ c. laid-back and relaxed   ___ f. shy and reserved   ___ i. neat and tidy

B **Pair work** Choose another partner. Find two traits you have in common. Find one way that you're different.

"So, how would you describe yourself?"

"Well, I'd say I'm pretty laid-back and relaxed."

"Me too. I never worry about getting places on time."

"I don't either. I like taking it easy and . . ."

Useful expressions	
Same traits	**Different traits**
So am I. (I am too.)	I'm not like that.
I'm the same way.	I'd say I'm more . . .
So do I. (I do too.)	Really? I don't.
Neither do I. (I don't either.)	That's not true for me.

3 Verbs followed by gerunds

grammar

Use the gerund form after these verbs.
I **enjoy going** to parties where I don't know everyone.
I **avoid expressing** my feelings and ideas in public.
I **don't mind giving up** my time to help other people.

Use the gerund or infinitive form after these verbs.
I **can't stand being / to be** in a messy room.
I **love taking / to take** my friends to cool new clubs.
I **hate getting up / to get up** for early morning classes.

Use the gerund form after these expressions containing prepositions.
I **insist on making** my own decisions.
I always **feel like going** dancing!
I'm **into going** out to new foreign restaurants.

Grammar Plus: See page 106.

A Look at the starting point on page 2 again. Can you find other expressions that are followed by gerunds? Which of them can also be followed by infinitives?

B **Pair work** How do you feel about these things? Discuss your answers using verbs or expressions followed by gerunds and infinitives.

1. tell people that I'm angry with them
2. help with chores around the house
3. listen to people's personal problems
4. stay out late the night before an interview
5. start conversations with people I don't know
6. go to places where I have to use my English

"I usually avoid telling people that I'm angry with them. I guess I'm just afraid of making them even angrier."

4 Personal profiles

speaking

A Look at the information about these people. Which person is most similar to you?

Meet Your Neighbors

	Wendy	Carlo	Linda	Chris
Job	college student	artist	lawyer	teacher
Personality	friendly and outgoing	wild and crazy	shy and reserved	laid-back and relaxed
Lifestyle	• loves playing sports • into traveling	• loves to dance • can't stand going home early	• into watching old movies	• enjoys cooking meals for friends • loves to tell jokes

B **Group work** Write a similar profile for yourself. Don't write your name. Your teacher will take your profile and give you another. Ask questions around the class to find the writer.

5 Changes

listening

A 🔘 Listen to Marcos and Heather talk about how they have changed over the last five years. How did they change? Complete the chart with the expressions from the box.

| kind and generous | friendly and outgoing | shy and reserved | wild and crazy |

	used to be . . .	has become . . .
Marcos		
Heather		

B 🔘 Listen again. Which person do you think would be more likely to do these things this weekend? Check (✓) Marcos or Heather.

	Marcos	Heather
1. stay out late at a big party	☐	☐
2. stay home and watch TV	☐	☐
3. help a relative with a personal problem	☐	☐
4. invite a classmate to a funny movie	☐	☐

6 How have you changed?

discussion

A How have you changed over the last five years? What do you want to change now? Complete the chart.

	How I've changed	How I'd like to change
Habits		
Personality		
Likes and dislikes		

B **Pair work** Compare your charts. Ask follow-up questions.

"*I used to watch a lot of TV. Now I don't.*"

"*Really? What made you change?*"

"*Well, I was afraid of getting out of shape. So I . . .*"

Useful expressions

Describing how you've changed	**Describing how you'd like to change**
I used to . . . , but now I . . .	I'd like to be more . . .
I think I've become more . . .	I'm interested in . . .

7 Topic sentences

writing

> The main idea is usually found in the first sentence of the paragraph. This sentence is called the topic sentence.

A Read these paragraphs about people's best and worst qualities. Underline the topic sentence in each paragraph.

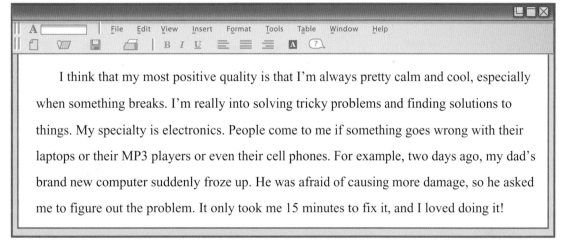

I think that my most positive quality is that I'm always pretty calm and cool, especially when something breaks. I'm really into solving tricky problems and finding solutions to things. My specialty is electronics. People come to me if something goes wrong with their laptops or their MP3 players or even their cell phones. For example, two days ago, my dad's brand new computer suddenly froze up. He was afraid of causing more damage, so he asked me to figure out the problem. It only took me 15 minutes to fix it, and I loved doing it!

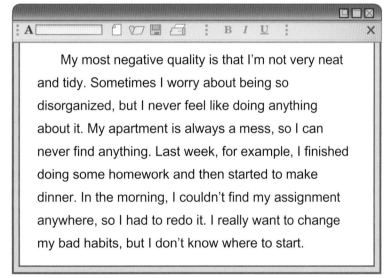

My most negative quality is that I'm not very neat and tidy. Sometimes I worry about being so disorganized, but I never feel like doing anything about it. My apartment is always a mess, so I can never find anything. Last week, for example, I finished doing some homework and then started to make dinner. In the morning, I couldn't find my assignment anywhere, so I had to redo it. I really want to change my bad habits, but I don't know where to start.

B Think about your own personal qualities. Make a list. Then decide which quality is most positive and which is most negative. Circle each one.

C Write a paragraph about either your most positive or your most negative quality. Make sure your paragraph has only one main idea.

D **Pair work** Exchange paragraphs with a partner. Then answer the questions.

1. What is your partner's topic sentence? Underline it.

2. What examples did your partner give?

3. What did you find most interesting about your partner's paper?

Different types of families

starting point

A Look at the families in the pictures. What's different about each type of family?

What's Your Family Like?

The Watsons, Sydney

"My wife and I both work now, and the extra money is great. The only trouble with being a **two-income family** is we don't spend as much time together."

The Wangs, Vancouver

"We're an **extended family** now that Grandma has moved in. The big advantage of having her at home is that she can baby-sit more often."

The Patels, London

"We're a typical **nuclear family** – it's just my sister, my parents, and me. The only bad thing about living in our house is there's only one bathroom!"

B **Pair work** What are some more advantages and disadvantages of each type of family? Compare ideas.

"In a nuclear family, you might not see your grandparents every day. That's a disadvantage."

How are their families different?

listening & speaking

A Listen to Paul and Andrea talk about their families. What kind of family did each person grow up in? How have their families changed?

B Listen again. Match the people on the left with the phrases on the right.

1. Andrea __b__
2. Andrea's husband ____
3. Andrea's sister-in-law ____
4. Paul's sister ____
5. Paul ____
6. Paul's mother ____

a. has two daughters.
b. doesn't know her in-laws very well.
c. has three brothers.
d. is looking forward to seeing the family.
e. will be cooking for 12 people.
f. is a law student.

C **Pair work** Is your family similar to Paul's or Andrea's? How is it similar? How is it different?

grammar

A noun clause is a part of a sentence that has both a subject and a predicate. *That* is optional in noun clauses after *be*. Also notice the prepositions used in each sentence.

The only trouble **with** being a two-income family is **(that) we don't spend as much time together**.
The big advantage **of** having Grandma at home is **(that) she can baby-sit more often**.

Grammar Plus: See page 107.

A Look at the starting point on page 6 again. Can you find the noun clause in the last example? Which preposition is used in the first part of the sentence?

B Combine the sentences. Then compare answers with a partner.

1. I'm the youngest in the family. The nice thing is I get a lot of attention.
   The nice thing about being the youngest in the family is that I get a lot of attention.
2. I have a younger sister. The trouble is she always wants to borrow my clothes.
3. I'm away at college. The bad part is that I miss my family.
4. I work at night. The worst thing is I can't have dinner with my family.
5. I'm the oldest in the family. One bad thing is that I always have to baby-sit.

C Complete the sentences with your own ideas.
Then compare answers with a partner.

1. An advantage of being a twin is . . .
   that you always have someone to hang out with.
2. A problem with being an only child is . . .
3. One benefit of being the oldest is . . .
4. A big disadvantage of having an older sibling is . . .
5. The best thing about having a big family is . . .

 Family matters

discussion

A Check (✓) at least three questions you'd like to talk about with your group.

- ☐ What's the best thing about spending time with your family? What's the worst thing?
- ☐ What's one advantage of having a close family?
- ☐ What are some rules that people have to follow in your family?
- ☐ What's a benefit of having strict parents?
- ☐ Are you most likely to confide in a parent, a sibling, or a friend?
- ☐ Do you believe mothers and fathers should do the same chores?
- ☐ What are the advantages and disadvantages of having a two-income family?

B **Group work** Discuss the questions you chose. Ask follow-up questions and make sure everyone in your group participates.

5 Compound family terms

vocabulary

A Match the family members on the left with the definitions on the right.

1. Your great-aunt is ____
2. Your granddaughter is ____
3. Your sister-in-law is ____
4. Your great-grandmother is ____

a. your father's or mother's grandmother.
b. your mother's or father's aunt.
c. your son's or daughter's daughter.
d. your wife's or husband's sister, or your brother's wife.

B Which of the family members in the box can be combined with a prefix or suffix in the chart? Complete the chart with a partner. What does each term mean?

aunt	daughter	mother	niece	son
brother	father	nephew	sister	uncle

great-	grand-	great-grand-	-in-law
aunt	daughter	mother	sister

"Your great-nephew is your brother's or sister's grandson."

6 Family reunion

listening

A 🔘 Listen to Victor tell a friend about his family reunion. What were they celebrating at the reunion?

B 🔘 Listen again. In addition to immediate family, what other relatives of Victor's were there? Check (✓) the people you hear mentioned.

☐ 1. his grandfather   ☐ 4. his sister-in-law   ☐ 7. his mother-in-law

☐ 2. his uncle's cousin   ☐ 5. his niece   ☐ 8. his cousin

☐ 3. his brother   ☐ 6. his son   ☐ 9. friends of the family

7 The more, the merrier

A **Group work** What's the size of an average family where you're from? Discuss with your group.

FULL HOUSE : Meet the Silcocks

Walk into the California home of Anne Belles and her husband, Jim Silcock, and you'll see kids everywhere playing video games, doing homework, and getting ready for dinner. There are 30 boys in this close-knit household and Anne Belles is their mom. Belles has wanted to help children since she was a kid. "I was intrigued by the movie *Oliver!* in the '60s, a musical based on the Charles Dickens novel *Oliver Twist.* I told my mom, 'That's what I want to do. I want to adopt orphans.'"

Anne's boys range in age from 3 to 25. All of them are challenged in some way. "They each have special needs – physically, emotionally, or at school," says Belles. She doesn't focus on what her kids can't do, only on what they can. They go to mainstream schools, take karate, go skating at the roller rink, and even act on television. In an interesting twist, thirteen of her boys are going to be in a local theater's production of *Oliver!*

Raising 30 boys is no small task. Every day, a small army of childcare workers, nurses, and volunteers comes in to help cook and clean, wash 30 loads of laundry a day, and take care of health needs.

To find out how much such a large family costs, we followed Jim Silcock to the grocery store. He spent $880.00 for food for one week. Every month they spend $2,000 to run five mini-vans, $15,000 for the fourteen paid helpers, and more than $10,000 on dental and medical expenses. There's also clothing, insurance and mortgage payments.

The family receives $26,000 a month from the federal government, and has some income from a family business. All the money is spent on the children; having new clothes and fancy cars isn't important to Belles.

How do the kids feel? Says 17-year-old Anthony, "The family is there whenever I need something . . . . Under all this chaos, I feel like I am loved."

"This was my dream. And everything about what I'm doing was everything I wanted to happen in my life," says Anne Belles. "So, absolutely no regrets; this is perfect. I couldn't ask for it to be better – maybe a bigger house, you know, would be nice."

Source: "Full House: Meet the Silcocks," by Steve Kroft, CBS News Archives

B Read the article and answer the questions. Then compare answers with a partner.

1. What reason does Anne Belles give for adopting so many children?

2. What's special about the children that Belles and her husband adopt?

3. What are the total monthly expenses for this family?

C **Group work** Discuss these questions. Then share your answers with the class.

1. What do you think would be the best thing about living in this family?

2. Would you like to be in a family as large as the Silcocks'?

Mistakes and mysteries

LESSON A · Life lessons

1 Learning the hard way

starting point

A Read about these people's problems. What mistake did each person make?

What Did I Get Myself Into?
Three mistakes that led to big messes

I was supposed to be studying this weekend for a math test. But my friends made me go to the beach with them instead. I mean, I didn't have to go with them, but I did. Now the test is in two hours, and I'm totally unprepared. I should have stayed home and studied!
-Alicia, Orizaba, Mexico

In high school, I had to wear a uniform, so I didn't have a lot of fashionable clothes. When I started college, I thought I needed to have more, so I wasted a lot of money on trendy outfits. But I really shouldn't have done it. Now I'm broke!
-Kenichi, Osaka, Japan

We weren't supposed to cook in our dorm rooms, but I had a microwave anyway. The cafeteria was right next door, so I really didn't need to have it. Anyway, I got caught making popcorn last week, and the school took the microwave away.
-Melanie, Toronto, Canada

B Pair work What should each person do differently in the future? Compare ideas.

"I don't think Alicia should listen to her friends in the future."

"Yeah, I agree. She shouldn't have let them influence her like that."

2 I'll never do that again!

listening

A 💿 Listen to Frank talk about a bad decision he made. What was his decision? Why was it a bad one?

B 💿 Listen again. Are these statements true or false? Check (✓) the correct answer.

	True	False
1. Frank and his neighbor were good friends.	☐	☐
2. Frank knew he was allergic to cats.	☐	☐
3. Frank marked his calendar to remember to feed the cat.	☐	☐
4. Frank forgot what time his train was going to leave.	☐	☐
5. Frank remembered to feed the cat on Saturday.	☐	☐

3 Past modals and phrasal modals of obligation

grammar

Should have, **was supposed to**, **had to**, and *needed to* all describe obligations in the past, although they sometimes have different uses.

I **should have** stayed home and studied! (It was a good idea, but I didn't do it.)
I **was supposed to** be studying this weekend. (It was required, but I didn't do it.)
I **had to** wear a uniform. (We were forced to do this.)
I **didn't have to** go with my friends, but I did. (There was no obligation.)
I thought I **needed to** have more clothes. (I thought this was necessary.)

Grammar Plus: See page 108.

A Look at the starting point on page 10 again. Can you find other examples of past modals and phrasal modals of obligation? What does each one mean?

B Choose the answer that best describes what these sentences mean. Then compare answers with a partner.

1. I shouldn't have invited them.
   a. I didn't invite them.
   b. I invited them.

2. That was a secret! You weren't supposed to tell anyone!
   a. You didn't tell anyone.
   b. You told someone.

3. We didn't have to study for the test.
   a. We forgot to study.
   b. We were prepared for the test.

4. I know Jane didn't like my cooking, but she didn't need to be so rude about it.
   a. Jane was rude to me.
   b. Jane wasn't rude to me.

C Complete the sentences with information about yourself. Then compare answers with a partner.

1. After I started high school, I had to . . .

   I had to study a lot harder.

2. I made someone angry once because I wasn't supposed to . . .

3. I wasted a lot of money once because I thought I needed to . . .

4. When I had the opportunity, I should have . . .

4 Past experiences

discussion

A Look at the survey and check the items that are true for you.

Have you ever . . .

- ☐ enjoyed doing something you weren't supposed to do?
- ☐ not done something you should have done?
- ☐ done something foolish that you didn't need to do?
- ☐ had to follow a rule you didn't like?
- ☐ had to enforce a rule you didn't like?

B **Pair work** Discuss your answers. Ask follow-up questions.

"Have you ever enjoyed doing something you weren't supposed to do?"

"Sure. At my old job, I wasn't supposed to take a long lunch. But I took long lunches at the park, anyway. How about you?"

5. Recognizing problems

vocabulary

A These verbs are often used to talk about problems. Use the verbs to replace the boldfaced words and phrases in the sentences below.

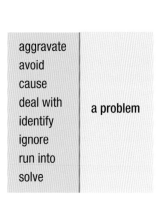

aggravate	
avoid	
cause	
deal with	**a problem**
identify	
ignore	
run into	
solve	

1. My friend **never does anything about** his problems.
   My friend always ignores his problems.
2. Maria can look at a broken bicycle and **find** the problem right away.
3. My sister is never afraid to **try to take care of** a difficult problem.
4. Gil Dong always **makes** his problems **worse**.
5. Ruby always follows the recipe closely to **prevent** problems when she cooks.
6. Ming always **unexpectedly encounters** problems when he tries to fix things.
7. Carla is great at **completely fixing** any kind of problem at work.
8. Al is the kind of student who always **makes** problems for teachers.

B **Pair work** Do you know anyone similar to the people in the sentences above? Tell your partner.

"My cousin always ignores her problems. Her car is always making strange noises, but she never does anything about it."

6. Dealing with problems

listening

A Listen to Ray (*R*), Felipe (*F*), and Jennifer (*J*) talk about a problem that they each had. What did each person finally do about the problem? Write the correct letter.

____ ignore it   ____ deal with it   ____ aggravate it

B Listen again. Briefly describe each person's problem.

Ray: _____

Felipe: _____

Jennifer: _____

7 Brainstorming

writing

> *Brainstorming* means making a list of ideas about a topic. Then you can use this list to come up with a topic sentence and ideas to support it.

A Group work Brainstorm as many ideas as you can to add to the example below.

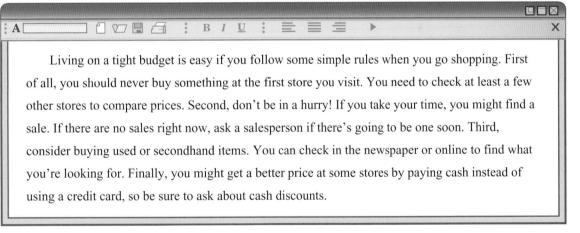

Living on a Tight Budget

Do	Don't
• compare prices	• buy the first thing you see
• look for sales	• buy brand names
• check classified ads for used items	• use credit cards

B Group work Brainstorm dos and don'ts for one of these topics. Write your ideas.

- getting over a bad cold
- staying safe in a big city
- preparing for entrance exams

C Now write a topic sentence and a paragraph using your ideas.

> Living on a tight budget is easy if you follow some simple rules when you go shopping. First of all, you should never buy something at the first store you visit. You need to check at least a few other stores to compare prices. Second, don't be in a hurry! If you take your time, you might find a sale. If there are no sales right now, ask a salesperson if there's going to be one soon. Third, consider buying used or secondhand items. You can check in the newspaper or online to find what you're looking for. Finally, you might get a better price at some stores by paying cash instead of using a credit card, so be sure to ask about cash discounts.

D Pair work Exchange brainstorming lists and paragraphs with a partner. Then answer the questions.

1. How many brainstorming ideas did your partner use? Do you think he or she chose the best ones?

2. Do you have any questions about your partner's paragraph? Is there anything you disagree with?

3. Can you think of a good title for your partner's paragraph? Explain your choice.

1. Do you have any guesses?

starting point

A Read the news story and the comments to the right. Which comments do you agree with?

Cartoon-Based Illness Mystifies Japan

TOKYO – More than 700 children were rushed to hospitals Tuesday after suffering convulsions, vomiting, and irritated eyes after watching a popular Japanese cartoon.

The network said it plans to cancel next week's show if the cause of the incident remains unclear.

 Most of the children developed the symptoms after a scene featuring five seconds of flashing red light in the eyes of the show's most popular character.

TV executive Hironari Mori said the scene passed inspection before broadcast, but in hindsight "we believe there may have been problems."

"As an adult that part made me blink, so for a child the effect must have been considerable," Mori said.

Dr. Yukio Fukuyama, an expert on the brain, said that "television epilepsy" can be triggered by flashing, colorful lights. Fukuyama says parents should be made aware of the danger. "The networks should definitely think of issuing a health warning beforehand," he said.

"The children must have been totally immersed in the program," psychologist Rika Kayama said.

Source: "Cartoon-Based Illness Mystifies Japan," Reuters

Reader Comments

Yuki52: I'm certain the flashing lights must have caused the seizures.

MikeNYC: It could have been the flashing lights, but I'm not sure.

Paulo2008: The parents shouldn't have let their kids watch so much TV.

Soon_Hee: The seizures might have been caused by stress.

TeacherJim: That TV executive must have felt pretty embarrassed.

ChicagoMom: The children shouldn't have been sitting so close to the TV!

MGarcia: The TV network should have been more careful.

More >>

B Pair work Compare your reactions to the story.

"I'm certain the flashing lights must have caused the seizures."

"I don't know. It could have been the flashing lights, but I'm not sure."

2 Modals with multiple uses

To express degrees of certainty, use *must (not), can't, could (not), might (not),* or *may (not).*
I'm certain the flashing lights **must have caused** the seizures.
The seizures **might have been caused** by stress.

To express obligation, advice, or opinions, use *should (not).* Do not use *must (not) have* for obligations, advice, or opinions about the past.
The TV network **should have been** more careful. (obligation)
The networks **should think** of issuing a health warning. (advice)
The children **shouldn't have been sitting** so close to the TV! (opinion)

Also notice how these modals are used in the passive and continuous.

Grammar Plus: See page 109.

A Look at the starting point on page 14 again. What does each modal express? Which ones are used in the passive?

B Use modals to write reactions to these situations. Then compare answers with a partner.

1. You and your friend planned to meet, but your friend never arrived.

   He might have been busy at work. But he should have called to say he couldn't meet.

2. You loaned your classmate a lot of money last week, but she still hasn't repaid you.

3. You feel sick after a big fish dinner.

4. You receive flowers from a secret admirer.

5. You haven't received any phone calls in a week.

6. Your boss promised to promote you, but it still hasn't happened.

3 What's the explanation?

A Read these headlines about strange events. How would you explain them?

Mysterious light seen over Arizona

PHOENIX – Authorities are baffled by dozens of reports yesterday of strange and mysterious lights in the sky and unidentified flying objects over the desert. Por~ ~~ ~~ny as five

Loch Ness Monster Found?

INVERNESS, SCOTLAND – Another round of monster fever has hit the area with the release of more photographs that seem ~~

Monster raising its e~ head over the surfac Tourists and true bel~ flo~

Strange patterns found in wheat crops

KANSAS CITY – Local residents are scratching their heads over the | over the sudden appearance of large, complex circular

B Group work Discuss your explanations.

"That light must have been a UFO. I mean, it doesn't look like a normal plane."

"I know what you mean, but it might have been an unusual storm or something."

Useful expressions

Disagreeing
I don't know.
I'm not so sure.
Well, maybe, but . . .
I know what you mean, but . . .

4 Verbs of belief

A Put these verbs of belief in the columns. Discuss your answers with a partner.

| assume | be positive | bet | figure | have a hunch | suppose |
| be certain | be sure | doubt | guess | know for a fact | suspect |

Certain	Not certain

B **Group work** Use the verbs of belief to discuss these questions.

1. Why do giraffes have long necks?
2. Why do some buildings not have a thirteenth floor?
3. Is there intelligent life on other planets?
4. What should you do if you get sprayed by a skunk?
5. What color is an insect's blood?
6. Why doesn't a haircut hurt?

"Why do giraffes have long necks?"

"I'm not sure, but I assume they have long necks to eat the leaves at the tops of trees."

"Yeah, I bet that's the reason why."

5 Still unsolved mysteries

A Do you think that things like UFOs and alien abductions really happen?

B Listen to a radio program about a famous claim of alien abduction in Canada. What did the Hills say happened to them?

C Listen again. Check (✓) the facts or claims that the people mention. Which ones support the Hills' story? Which ones don't?

☐ 1. The Hills saw an object flying beside their car.
☐ 2. Betty saw creatures looking at them from the object.
☐ 3. The creatures spoke to the Hills in a strange language.
☐ 4. Betty found pink powder on her dress the next day.
☐ 5. The Air Force agreed that Betty saw a UFO.
☐ 6. The doctors doubted the Hills' story.
☐ 7. The aliens looked just like creatures from a TV show.
☐ 8. The trip took seven hours instead of four.

D **Group work** What do you think really happened to the Hills? Why? Discuss your reasons.

6. Do I know you?

A Group work What does *amnesia* mean? What are some things that might cause amnesia? Discuss with your group.

Amnesia *Spoils* Newlyweds' Bliss

What if the person you married forgot who you were? For one Texas couple, marriage became a blind date when the groom came down with amnesia days after their wedding.

Amy and Sean McNulty's wedding day started well, but ended with a shock. One of Sean's good friends was in a coma because of a serious car accident. Nevertheless, Amy and Sean decided to make their honeymoon trip according to plans.

At the airport, Sean realized he'd left his wallet in their car after they'd parked. He said to Amy, "I'll be right back." But he didn't return.

Amy contacted the police, who found Sean wandering near a motel three days later. He was confused and covered in bug bites. He had no idea who he was or who Amy was. Sean could not remember any personal details from his life, not even his mother.

Amy was now married to a man who viewed her as a stranger. "I wondered, you know, is he going to remember me? How is our relationship going to work?" said Amy.

This was a big change after a six-year courtship and plenty of shared memories.

"I had to learn to ask him, 'Can I hug you?' I mean, that was hard," said Amy.

Psychiatrist Dr. Daniel Brown says Sean's amnesia might have been caused by a series of stressful moments, like his friend's car accident. According to Dr. Brown, Sean's brain didn't connect with his identity anymore. "He doesn't know who Sean McNulty is and has no memories to help."

"It's sort of like if you forgot the name of a file you stored on your computer. You know it's there but you can't find it," said Brown. "His memory is like that."

Fortunately, the better times soon arrived. The day before their first anniversary, Sean's memories flooded back in an instant. He soon remembered everything, including their wedding. "I remember shoving cake in her face," said Sean. "It was great."

Sean views the experience as a chance to confirm he picked the right bride. "I got to see how much she loves me," said Sean. "We have a much stronger, closer bond from the experience. I couldn't have found a better woman to spend my life with."

Source: "Amnesia Spoils Newlyweds' Bliss," ABC News

B Read the article. Are these statements true or false? Check (✓) the correct answer.

	True	False
1. Sean's amnesia began after he was in a serious car accident.	☐	☐
2. Sean shoved cake in Amy's face when he remembered who she was.	☐	☐
3. The amnesia might have been caused by too much stress.	☐	☐

C Group work Discuss these questions. Then share your answers with the class.

1. What do you personally think might have caused Sean's amnesia?
2. What would you do if you were in Amy's position?

Exploring new cities

1 Cities of the world

starting point

A Read about these cities. Which city would you most like to visit?

BARCELONA

Barcelona is famous for museums, nightlife, and seafood – and for the architect Antoni Gaudí, who designed several of the city's most distinctive buildings. The restaurants here stay open until midnight, when many locals are still enjoying dinner.

BEIJING

Beijing has many popular tourist attractions, which include the Great Wall of China, the Summer Palace, and the Forbidden City. Tourists who come here for the first time are amazed by the crowds, the busy streets, and the constantly changing skyline.

The place where most tourists go first in Sydney is the famous Opera House, but this Australian city also has great restaurants and museums. The spring and fall are the seasons when most people come to visit.

Seoul is well known for its spicy food and its shopping areas, where you can find everything from antique pottery to custom-made clothing. The Myeong-dong area has dozens of shops that sell the latest fashions.

SYDNEY

SEOUL

B **Pair work** Tell your partner about a city you know.

"I know Vancouver. It's got the ocean on one side and mountains on the other. It's really beautiful, but it's expensive . . . "

2 Where in the world . . . ?

listening

A Listen to Diana and Matt talk about two cities. Who is talking about Athens and who is talking about Seoul?

B Listen again. Who mentions these topics, Diana (*D*) or Matt (*M*)? Write the correct letter.

___ 1. founded 3,000 years ago	___ 4. architecture	___ 7. traffic
___ 2. delicious, spicy food	___ 5. subway system	___ 8. street vendors
___ 3. beautiful beaches	___ 6. monuments	___ 9. nightlife

3 Defining and non-defining relative clauses

grammar

A defining relative clause defines or gives essential information about a noun.
The Myeong-dong area has dozens of shops **that sell the latest fashions**.
The spring and fall are the seasons **when most people come to visit**.

A non-defining relative clause gives optional information about a noun and cannot begin
with the pronoun *that*. Notice the use of commas.
The restaurants here stay open until midnight, **when many locals are still enjoying dinner**.
Beijing has many popular tourist attractions, **which include the Great Wall of China**.

Grammar Plus: See page 110.

A Look at the starting point on page 18 again. Can you find more relative clauses?

B Underline the relative clauses in the sentences and add commas where
necessary. Write *D* for a defining and *ND* for a non-defining relative clause.

ND 1. Bangkok, <u>which is the capital of Thailand</u>, has many
excellent restaurants and markets.

___ 2. Hong Kong was a British colony until 1997 when it
was returned to China.

___ 3. Busan is a busy port city that is located in South Korea.

___ 4. Bogotá which is situated on a high plateau in central
Colombia has frequently changing weather.

___ 5. Montreal is a sophisticated city where some of the
best cuisine in Canada is found.

___ 6. São Paulo which is the biggest city in Brazil is also
one of the world's most populated cities.

C Join the sentences using non-defining relative clauses. Then compare answers.

1. Gaudí also designed Barcelona's Park Güell. You can see fabulous sculptures there.

2. Seoul's name comes from the ancient word *Seorabeol*. *Seorabeol* means capital.

3. The center of Beijing is Tiananmen Square. It is the world's largest public square.

4. A great time to visit Seoul is in the fall. This is when Korean people celebrate
the Chuseok festival.

5. Japanese restaurants are now popular in Barcelona. They have started appearing
in recent years.

6. Australia's first European settlers came to Sydney in the 1700s. They were originally
from Great Britain.

4 A great place to visit

speaking

A Which of the cities on page 18 would you like to visit? Write three sentences
explaining your reasons. Use relative clauses where appropriate.

Barcelona is a city that I'd like to visit because . . .

B **Pair work** Tell your partner which city you'd like to visit and why.

5 What makes a city?

vocabulary

A Are these features of cities more important to tourists or to residents? Put the words in the columns. Add ideas of your own.

| climate | crime rate | green spaces | job market | neighborhoods | shopping |
| cost of living | cuisine | hotels | landmarks | nightlife | transportation system |

Important to tourists	Important to residents	Important to both

B **Pair work** Use the features above to talk about your city. Give examples and add extra information.

"Salvador is famous all over Brazil for its cuisine. Acarajé is one of the most popular foods, and it's really delicious. It's a deep-fried cake that's made from mashed beans."

6 What's the city like?

listening

A Listen to Carlos and Vicki talk about San Francisco. Who seems to like the city better?

B Listen again. Check (✓) the city features that Carlos and Vicki mention.

- ☐ 1. climate
- ☐ 2. architecture
- ☐ 3. shopping
- ☐ 4. customs
- ☐ 5. hotels
- ☐ 6. job market
- ☐ 7. landmarks
- ☐ 8. nightlife
- ☐ 9. cuisine

7 Perfect places

discussion

A Answer the questions with your own ideas.

What is...

1. a good city for budget travelers? _____
2. a good city for a honeymoon? _____
3. a place that would make a great family vacation spot? _____
4. a city where you'd like to live for a few years? _____
5. a good city to go to school in? _____
6. a place that you would never want to visit? _____

B **Pair work** Discuss your answers.

"I think New York is a good place for budget travelers."

"I'm not sure I agree. New York is incredibly expensive."

"That's true, but there are lots of cheap fast-food restaurants . . ."

Useful expressions	
Agreeing with an opinion	**Disagreeing with an opinion**
I think you're right.	I'm not sure I agree.
I'm with you.	Maybe, but don't you think . . . ?
That's true.	Really?
I think so too.	I know what you mean, but . . .

C **Group work** Join another pair and try to agree on one answer for each question.

8. Organizing ideas

writing

> Making a mind map is a good way of organizing your brainstorming ideas.
> Mind maps help you map out the supporting details about your topic.

A Look at the phrases in the box about Cuzco, Peru. Choose the main idea and
write it in the center of the mind map. Then write the supporting details in
the mind map.

beautiful architecture	wonderful restaurants	nice hotels
something for everyone	great shopping	a mix of history and culture

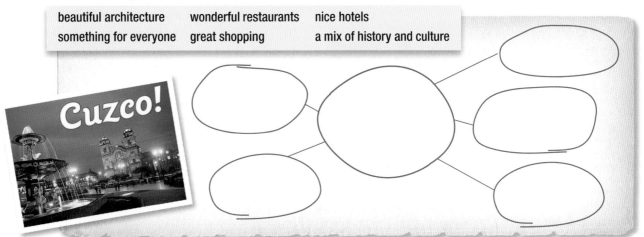

B Read the paragraph about Cuzco. Underline the ideas
from the mind map in the paragraph.

Machu Picchu

Cuzco has something for everyone. It's the oldest
city in the Americas, and it was once the capital of
the Inca empire. Today, Cuzco is Peru's tourist
capital because of its interesting mix of history
and culture. People who are interested in
architecture will love the nearby Inca ruins of
Machu Picchu and the palace of Inca Roqa. Cuzco
has many places to stay, which range from first-
class hotels to cozy inns. There are also many cafés
and restaurants where you can eat unique local dishes or international cuisine. Also,
Cuzco has great markets where you can shop for Indian art and local crafts. When
you visit Cuzco, you should try to experience all it has to offer.

C Choose a place you know and make your own mind map. Be sure the main
idea is general and contains several supporting ideas.

D Write a paragraph based on the ideas in your mind map.

E **Pair work** Exchange paragraphs with a partner. Then answer the questions.

1. Is there any information you would like your partner to add?

2. Does the content of the paragraph reflect the ideas in the mind map?

3. Would you like to visit the place your partner wrote about? Why or why not?

1 City search

starting point

A Complete the descriptions with the sentences below. Then compare answers.

◄ **This exciting large city** with bustling streets is a great place to live. Most evenings you can choose from a movie, a concert, or even a museum. (1) _____ There are lots of jobs here, and the average salary is about $3,000 per month. (2) _____ Our efficient new subway system can get you anywhere you want to go. (3) _____

This is a picturesque little resort town ▶ with year-round outdoor activities. There's something to do in all four seasons. But there's not much action here at night. (4) _____ There are many quaint little stores and boutiques. (5) _____ Apartments are affordable too. You can get a great place for about $1,000 a month, and average monthly salaries are about $2,500. (6) _____

a. However, housing costs are high. A nice apartment is about $2,500 per month.

b. So, even though our streets are safe, the evenings can be dull.

c. But be careful – in spite of all the late-night activity, the crime rate is high.

d. On the other hand, it can sometimes be difficult to find a job.

e. Although it's fast, clean, and cheap, it's pretty crowded during rush hour. Nevertheless, it's still the most popular way for people to get to work.

f. Despite the nearby shops, you'll still want a car. There are no buses here.

B **Pair work** Which city do you think has more to offer?

2 Compound terms for towns

vocabulary

A These compound terms describe different types of towns. How would you define each one?

border town	college town	mountain town	resort town	suburban town
coastal town	industrial town	port town	rural town	tourist town

A border town is near a border with another state or country.

B **Pair work** Which of the terms above best describes your hometown? Which best describes the town where you'd like to live someday? Compare ideas.

3 Order of modifiers

grammar

When two or more modifiers occur in a sentence, they usually follow this order.

	Quality	Size	Age	Type	Noun	Descriptive phrase
this	exciting	large			city	with bustling streets
a	picturesque	little		resort	town	with year-round outdoor activities
a	run-down		old	port	town	that has seen better days

Grammar Plus: See page 111.

A Look at the starting point on page 22 again. Can you find more sentences that have two or more modifiers?

B Write descriptions of places you know. Then compare answers with a partner.

1. a nearby city or town that you frequently visit

   Middleton is a typical suburban town with a good shopping mall.

2. a place you'd like to visit one day

3. a place tourists to your country want to see

4. a place you enjoy visiting, but wouldn't want to live in

4 Connecting contrasting ideas

grammar

You can use these words and phrases to connect contrasting ideas.

despite	although	however	on the other hand
in spite of	even though	nevertheless	

Grammar Plus: See page 111.

A Look at the starting point on page 22 again. What words and phrases connect the contrasting ideas?

B Circle the words that are true for you. Then complete the sentences.

1. Even though I (would) / *wouldn't* like to live in this town forever, . . .

   Even though I would like to live in this town forever, I'll have to move if the rents go up.

2. There are *not many / a lot of* things I like about this town. However, . . .

3. Although finding an apartment is *easy / difficult* in this town, . . .

4. Despite the high cost of living in this city, there are *a number of / no* . . .

5. The *spring / summer / fall / winter* here is very nice. On the other hand, . . .

6. Most places in this town close *early / late*. In spite of that, . . .

C **Pair work** Discuss your answers. Ask and answer follow-up questions.

"Even though I would like to live in this town forever, I'll have to move if the rents go up."
"Really? Where would you move?"
"I'm not sure. I hope someplace cheaper, but still near here."

5 Life in Sydney

A Listen to Maria and Ian talk about life in Sydney. Who seems to enjoy living there more?

B Listen again. Which person has these opinions? Check (✓) Maria, Ian, or both.

	Maria	Ian	Both
1. It's easy to get around Sydney.	☐	☐	☐
2. The beaches are great.	☐	☐	☐
3. The rents are expensive.	☐	☐	☐
4. It's a fun place to live.	☐	☐	☐
5. The restaurants are all expensive.	☐	☐	☐
6. Life is better in a smaller town.	☐	☐	☐

6 Quality of life

A Rate these quality-of-life issues as very important (✓✓), important (✓), or not important (✗). Can you add one more to the list?

Quality of Life

____ affordable housing   ____ first-class health care   ____ public transportation

____ a variety of restaurants   ____ historic neighborhoods   ____ varied retail shops

____ beautiful parks   ____ low crime rates   ____ wireless hot spots

____ exciting nightlife   ____ pleasant weather   _____

B **Pair work** How important are the points above in your town? Which three are the most important to you personally?

"I guess affordable housing and exciting nightlife are the most important to me. I'd love to find a place I could afford that was near someplace fun."

"I know what you mean. But for me, I guess low crime rates are probably the most important. I want to live somewhere where I feel safe. I don't mind if it's a little boring."

C **Class activity** Share your answers with your classmates. Which issues were mentioned most often?

7. Melbourne versus Sydney

reading

A **Pair work** What do you know about Melbourne and Sydney? Read the first two paragraphs. Then tell your partner.

A Tale of Two Cities

Welcome to the oldest rivalry in **Australia.**

Sydney has its Opera House and harbor. Melbourne has quaint old buildings and parks. Sydney has spectacular beaches, but Melbourne's are less crowded. Talk to Melbournians, and they'll say their city is best. Talk to Sydneysiders, and they'll say Sydney is the number one place to live.

According to many Melbournians, inhabitants live a life of ideas, discussion, and debate. People are active in the arts, and live well. Then again, that's what Sydneysiders say about their city, too.

Talk to Melbournians, and they'll tell you their city has friendlier and more outgoing people than Sydney. Most Sydneysiders won't disagree about their city being less friendly. Nevertheless, they'll be quick to tell you that it's a dynamic, world-class city with tons of things to do and see. Sydneysiders say they are always busy enjoying all that their city offers – such as the crashing surf at Bondi,

Bronte, or Manly Beaches; bushwalks through the Sydney Harbor National Park; or browsing in Paddington's colorful weekend market.

People in downtown Sydney are always on the move, rushing to make contacts, cutting deals, and gaining influence. In Melbourne, eating out is a pastime and the pace of life is slower and easier. Melbourne may not have the great surfing of Sydney, the beautiful Darling Harbor, or the Opera House; instead, it's low key and savvy. You have to dig a little to get under its surface, but once there, you'll find a perfect example of a chic, ultra-modern city. Sydney looks internationally for inspiration, but Melbourne tends to look regionally – to Japan, for example. In a word, if you were to compare them to American cities, Sydney would be sunny L.A., and Melbourne would be charming New York.

Source: "Melbourne and Sydney: A Tale of Two Cities," by Stephen Townsend and Simon Richard, Rough Guides

B Read the article again. Are these statements true or false? Check (✓) the correct answers.

	True	False
1. Both Melbournians and Sydneysiders love their city.	☐	☐
2. Melbourne is famous for its spectacular beaches.	☐	☐
3. The pace of life is slower for Sydneysiders than for Melbournians.	☐	☐
4. Melbourne gets ideas from different countries in Asia.	☐	☐

C **Group work** Discuss these questions. Then share your answers with the class.

1. Does Melbourne or Sydney seem more interesting to you?
2. Are there any cities in your country that have a rivalry? How are the cities different? How are the people different?

Communication review

Self-assessment

How well can you do these things? Rate your ability from 1 to 5 (1 = low, 5 = high).

Talk about likes and dislikes with verbs followed by gerunds (Ex. 1)   _____

Discuss problems in cities and ways to deal with them (Ex. 2)   _____

Understand stories about past mistakes (Ex. 3)   _____

Talk about past mistakes with past modals and phrasal modals (Ex. 3)   _____

Describe features of cities with relative clauses (Ex. 4)   _____

Now do the corresponding exercises below. Were your ratings correct?

 Likes and dislikes

discussion

A Look at these items. Can you think of a personal example for each one?

1. something you're into / not into doing by yourself
2. the kind of music you feel like listening to when you're in a bad mood
3. something you like doing when you're stressed out
4. a household chore you don't mind / can't stand doing
5. something you avoid doing, if possible

B **Pair work** Discuss your answers with a partner.

"I'm really into going to art galleries by myself. That way I can spend as much time as I want."

"Oh, I'm just the opposite. I don't really like going to galleries alone. It's nice to share the experience with someone."

 The people's action committee

discussion

A **Pair work** You are members of an action group that has been asked to suggest improvements for your city. Make a list of changes you think should be made.

"We think the city shouldn't allow cars in the downtown area on weekends. It would be nice to be able to walk around without worrying about traffic."

B **Group work** Compare your recommendations in groups. Choose the four most interesting recommendations and share them with the class.

Useful expressions

Making recommendations
The city should provide . . .
The city ought to . . . because . . .
Wouldn't it be nice if . . . ?
It would make a lot of sense to . . .

---

3. Who's sorry now?

A Listen to a radio show called *Who's Sorry Now?* What is the focus of the show? Check (✓) the correct answer.

☐ a. people's roommates in college

☐ b. things that people should or should not have done in the past

☐ c. family vacations

B 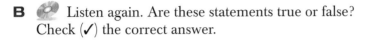 Listen again. Are these statements true or false? Check (✓) the correct answer.

	True	False
1. Mark made the manager think that Luke didn't want the job.	☐	☐
2. Mark said he should feel terrible, but he doesn't.	☐	☐
3. Anna buried her brother's harmonica in the desert.	☐	☐
4. Anna said she should have bought her brother a drum set.	☐	☐
5. Luke didn't tell his roommate that he knew about the call.	☐	☐
6. Luke said he should have told his roommate he knew about the call.	☐	☐

C Pair work Have you ever made a mistake like the ones on the radio show? Would you consider calling a show like *Who's Sorry Now?* to talk about it?

"Have you ever made a mistake like the ones on the radio show?"

"Well, when I was in college, I used to make up excuses so that I could avoid going to French class. I should have gone. I really wish I could speak French now."

"Would you call up a show like Who's Sorry Now?*"*

"I don't know. Maybe it would be fun. What about you?"

4. Welcome to my city

discussion

A What are three places in your city that people would enjoy visiting? Make a list.

B Group work Tell your group about your "must-see" places. Tell them why each place is worth seeing.

"Guadalajara, which is the second largest city in Mexico, has a lot of great markets. The Libertad Market is fantastic."

4 Early birds and night owls

LESSON A · It's about time!

1 What's your best time of day?

starting point

A Read these statements. How would you define the boldfaced words?

Teresa, South Africa

As soon as I get up in the morning, I race off to the gym. After I finish my workout, I head to the office. I always get there before any of my colleagues arrive. I suppose I'm a **morning person.**

Fausto, Brazil

Ever since I was a kid, I've had trouble getting up early, so I guess I'm a **late riser**. Until I've had my coffee, I'm such a grouch. I'm not very approachable right after I wake up!

Mieko, Japan

I'm a **power napper**. While I take my lunch break at work, I often sneak a five-minute nap at my desk. After I have a little sleep, I feel great the rest of the day.

Richard, Canada

I don't get much done until it gets to be late afternoon. Then I usually get a spurt of energy. I can concentrate best after everyone else has gone to bed. I'd say I'm a real **night owl**.

B **Group work** Which of the people above are you most similar to?

2 The time is right

discussion

A **Pair work** Read this information. Do you agree with the advice given?

When the Mind and Body Are at Their Best

 Whenever you need to study for a test, do it between **9:00 A.M. and noon**.

 Study languages in the **early afternoon**.

 Whenever you have to work with numbers, plan to do it around **noon**.

 Energy levels drop between **2:00 and 4:00 P.M.** Before your energy level falls, try taking a short nap.

 Do something that requires concentration between **6:00 and 9:00 P.M.**

 Your mind and body are sleepiest at **4:00 A.M.** This is why it's not a good idea to stay up studying all night.

Source: "The Secrets of Sleep," by Michael Segell, *Esquire*.

B **Pair work** Do you prefer to do these things in the morning, the afternoon, the evening, or at any time of the day? Compare answers.

1. exercise   2. listen to music   3. study for an exam   4. speak English

3 Reduced time clauses

grammar

Notice how these clauses show time relationships. If the subject of the sentence doesn't change, clauses with *(right) before*, *(right) after*, and *while* can be reduced.
After I finish / **After** finishing my workout, I head to the office.
While I take / **While** taking my lunch break at work, I often sneak a five-minute nap.
I'm not very approachable **right after** I wake up / **right after** waking up!

However, other time clauses cannot usually be reduced.
Ever since I was a kid, I've had trouble getting up early.
As soon as I get up in the morning, I race off to the gym.
Until I've had my coffee, I'm such a grouch.
Whenever you have to work with numbers, plan to do it around noon.
I've been a night person **from the moment** I started college.

Grammar Plus: See page 112.

A Look at the starting point and Exercise 2 on page 28 again. Can you find more time clauses? Which one can be reduced?

B **Pair work** Complete the sentences with information about yourself. Then discuss your answers with a partner.

1. While working on a really difficult task, . . .
2. I become really frustrated whenever . . .
3. I don't feel awake in the morning until . . .
4. Whenever I have trouble sleeping, . . .
5. I can never concentrate after . . .
6. From the moment I wake up in the morning . . .
7. After I've stayed out too late . . .
8. I take a nap whenever . . .

"While working on a really difficult task, I have to stretch every 30 minutes."

4 Energy and sleep

vocabulary & speaking

A Match the phrasal verb in the question with the correct definition.

1. Do you ever **burn out** from too much work? ____   a. become calm
2. How do you **calm down** after an argument? ____   b. find more energy
3. How do you **chill out** after a rough day? ____   c. go to bed
4. Do you **drop off** quickly after you go to bed? ____   d. lose all your energy
5. How do you **perk up** when you feel sleepy? ____   e. fall asleep
6. Do you **race off** as soon as class is over? ____   f. take it easy
7. How often do you **sleep over** at a friend's? ____   g. stay for the night
8. What time do you **turn in** on the weekend? ____   h. go quickly

B **Pair work** Discuss the questions above. Ask follow-up questions.

"Whenever I feel like I'm going to burn out, I go for a bike ride to relax."
"That sounds like a good idea. Where do you like to ride?"

5 Chilling out

A Stress can cause fatigue and a lack of energy. Check (✓) the things you do to cope with stress. Can you add other suggestions to the list?

- ☐ call a friend
- ☐ do vigorous exercise
- ☐ do yoga

- ☐ get a massage
- ☐ listen to music
- ☐ take a hot bath

- ☐ vent your feelings
- ☐ _____
- ☐ _____

B Listen to Sean (*S*), Lisa (*L*), and Victor (*V*) talk about stress. What is the main cause of stress for each person? Write the correct letter.

___ too little time ___ too much traffic ___ too many responsibilities

C Listen again. What solution has each person found? Complete the chart.

	Solution
1. Sean	
2. Lisa	
3. Victor	

6 I need some advice.

A Look at the problems below. Have you ever had a problem like this? What other problems do people have with sleep and energy levels?

Caller 1

I've been working day and night on an important project. It's going well, but I'm feeling so worn out. I'm worried about my health.

Caller 2

I get so nervous before I have to give a presentation that I can't sleep the night before, and then I'm not at my best.

Caller 3

I always put off studying until the night before the test. I stay up all night studying, but after that I still don't do very well.

Caller 4

Whenever my friends call me late at night, we talk for hours and hours. The next day, I can't keep my eyes open!

B **Pair work** Imagine you have one of the problems above. Take turns asking for and giving advice.

"I have a real problem. I've been working a lot on this project, and I'm so worn out. I'm worried about my health."

"So, how late do you usually work during the week?"

"I usually stay until 9:00 P.M. or so."

"Have you ever thought of telling someone that you need a little help?"

Useful expressions

Giving advice

Have you ever thought of (going) . . . ?
You might want to . . .
It might not be a bad idea to . . .
The way I see it, you ought to . . .

7 Effective topic sentences

writing

> Effective topic sentences are neither too general nor too specific. A topic sentence is supported by the other sentences in the paragraph.

A Read the paragraph and choose the best topic sentence from the list below.

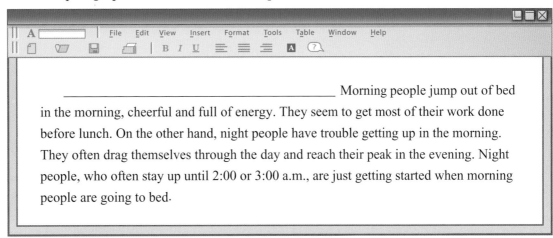

_____ Morning people jump out of bed in the morning, cheerful and full of energy. They seem to get most of their work done before lunch. On the other hand, night people have trouble getting up in the morning. They often drag themselves through the day and reach their peak in the evening. Night people, who often stay up until 2:00 or 3:00 a.m., are just getting started when morning people are going to bed.

a. Early mornings are bad times of day for most people.

b. Morning people and night people live very different lives.

c. Working at night is hard for morning people.

d. Night people get enough sleep even though they go to bed late.

B Read the paragraph and complete the topic sentence. Then compare your answers with a partner.

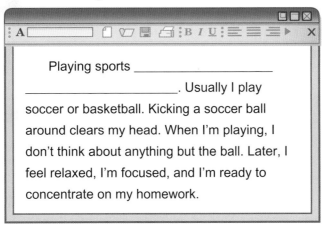

Playing sports _____
_____. Usually I play soccer or basketball. Kicking a soccer ball around clears my head. When I'm playing, I don't think about anything but the ball. Later, I feel relaxed, I'm focused, and I'm ready to concentrate on my homework.

C Choose one of these topics or your own idea. Then write a paragraph with a topic sentence.

- the best way to stay healthy
- an effective study plan
- earning extra money

D **Pair work** Take turns reading your paragraphs, but don't read the topic sentence. Can you guess what your partner's topic sentence is?

1 A good night's sleep

starting point

A Read the statements about sleep habits. Check (✓) the statements that are true for you.

> ☐ I sometimes lie awake at night, even if I'm really tired.
>
> ☐ I'm lucky I can get by on six hours of sleep, considering that most people need eight.
>
> ☐ I'm a light sleeper, so any little noise wakes me up unless I'm really tired.
>
> ☐ I can manage on five hours of sleep, as long as I take a nap during the day.
>
> ☐ Unless I get a good night's sleep, I can easily fall asleep at school, at work, or even while driving.
>
> ☐ I always set two alarm clocks just in case one of them doesn't go off.
>
> ☐ I only wake up early if I have somewhere to be in the morning.
>
> ☐ I never have any trouble sleeping.
>
> ☐ I'm exhausted every morning, even if I slept great all night.

B **Pair work** Compare your answers. Which statements did you check?

> "I definitely lie awake at night, even if I'm really tired. I can't help it. I replay everything that happened during the day."
>
> "You're not the only one. I do the same thing, especially when I'm feeling stressed."

2 Expressions related to sleep

vocabulary

A Put these expressions about sleep in the columns. Then compare answers.

be fast asleep	be wide awake	feel drowsy	nod off	take a power nap
be sound asleep	drift off	have a sleepless night	sleep like a log	toss and turn

Having trouble sleeping	Falling asleep	Sleeping a short time	Sleeping deeply
			be fast asleep

B **Pair work** Use the expressions to ask and answer questions.

> "Do you ever take a power nap during the day?"
>
> "Not really. Whenever I try to take a nap, I end up sleeping until the next morning. But let me ask you something. What do you do when you feel drowsy after lunch?"

3 Clauses stating reasons and conditions

grammar

Even if introduces a condition that does not influence the main clause.
I sometimes lie awake at night, **even if** I'm really tired.

Considering that introduces causes and reasons that explain the main clause.
I'm lucky I can get by on six hours of sleep, **considering that** most people need eight.

As long as introduces a condition on which the main clause depends.
I can manage on five hours of sleep, **as long as** I take a nap during the day.

Unless introduces something that must happen in order to avoid a consequence.
Unless I get a good night's sleep, I can easily fall asleep at school, at work, or even while driving.

(Just) in case introduces an undesirable circumstance that needs to be taken into account.
I always set two alarm clocks **(just) in case** one of them doesn't go off.

Only . . . if introduces a condition that must be met for the main clause to be true.
I **only** wake up early **if** I have somewhere to be in the morning.   *Grammar Plus: See page 113.*

A Look at the starting point on page 32 again. Can you find more clauses stating reasons and conditions?

B Match the clauses to make sentences. Then compare answers with a partner.

1. Drivers can fall asleep on the highway ____
2. Power naps at work are a good idea, ____
3. Some people just can't get to sleep ____
4. I was surprisingly alert at work, ____
5. Night owls hate to wake up early, ____
6. I only drink hot milk before bed ____

a. if I'm having trouble sleeping.
b. even if it's a beautiful morning.
c. unless they rest before long trips.
d. as long as you have the boss's OK.
e. considering that I didn't sleep at all last night.
f. unless they take a bath before bed.

C Complete the sentences with information about yourself. Then compare answers with a partner.

1. Unless I have enough sleep at night, . . .
   I can't think very clearly in the morning.
2. I usually wake up on time, as long as . . .
3. I fall asleep pretty quickly at night, considering that . . .
4. I always have a boring book on my night table just in case . . .
5. Even if I'm extremely stressed out, I never . . .
6. I only leave a light on if . . .

4. I had the wildest dream.

listening & speaking

A Listen to Kate and Sérgio talk about their recurring dreams. Whose dream do you think is scarier?

B Listen again. What is each person's dream? What do they think the dreams mean? Complete the chart.

	Dream	Meaning
Kate		
Sérgio		

C **Pair work** What do *you* think their dreams mean? Do you ever have similar dreams?

5. The meaning of dreams

discussion

A Read the information. Match the dreams with their meanings.

Dreams

1. **Falling** You are falling through space. Usually you don't hit the ground or hurt yourself. _____

2. **Flying** You are flying and enjoying the sensation. _____

3. **Being chased** You feel as if someone is chasing you and you're in danger. _____

4. **Being embraced** Someone you like approaches you and hugs you. _____

5. **Failing** Your teeth all fall out suddenly. _____

6. **Winning** You are successful in doing something. _____

7. **Being ashamed** You do something embarrassing and feel ashamed. _____

Meanings

a. You like someone and feel you can trust that person.

b. You feel very optimistic and proud about how your life is going.

c. You feel pleased with yourself and superior to other people.

d. You feel disappointed in yourself because of something you did.

e. You are worried about something, and this is a warning to be careful.

f. You feel out of control because someone is threatening you.

g. You feel insecure, and you are worried about losing something.

B **Pair work** Read these accounts of unusual dreams. What do you think they mean?

"Suddenly I found myself on stage in a school play and realized that I didn't know my lines. . . ."

"I was in a hot-air balloon above a big park. When I looked down, I was amazed to see hundreds of people on the ground pointing up at me. . . ."

"I was in a strange country and didn't know how I'd gotten there. I asked a man for help, and he held up a sign in a language I'd never seen before. . . ."

Useful expressions

Interpreting meaning
I think that means . . .
It sounds like . . .
The balloon probably stands for . . .
It might symbolize . . .

C **Group work** Finish each of the dreams above. Take turns adding sentences.

6 To sleep or not to sleep?

reading

A **Group work** Are there enough hours in the day to do everything you need to do? Discuss with your group. Then read the article.

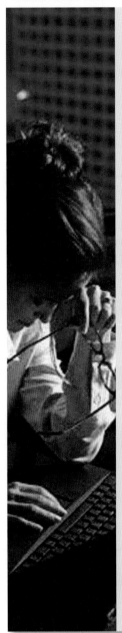

To Sleep or Not to Sleep?

In the days before electricity, people didn't worry much about sleep. They usually went to bed a couple of hours after sunset and woke at sunrise. After all, there wasn't much to do in those days after the sun went down. But then came the electric light bulb. And now we have satellite television, the Internet, 24-hour convenience stores, and longer hours at work. How much can we sleep? How much should we sleep?

Like it or not, many of us are sleeping less on average. In 1910, most Americans slept nine hours a night. That dropped to 7.5 hours by 1975. In 2002, a study by the National Sleep Foundation found that the average American got only 6.9 hours. The news is even worse for people who work the night shift. They sleep an average of just five hours.

Are we sleeping enough? Not if you believe in the old formula of eight hours of rest, eight hours of work, and eight hours of play. On the other hand, Norman Stanley, a British scientist who studies sleep, believes people's sleep needs vary. Some people need as many as 11 hours, but others need as few as three. How much do you really need? "To find out," he says, "simply sleep until you wake naturally, without the help of an alarm clock. That's your sleep need."

Meanwhile, other scientists and pharmaceutical researchers are searching for new ways to keep us awake longer. Some are developing chemicals that are safer and more powerful than caffeine, the chemical found in coffee and tea. One experimental drug, CX717, kept laboratory monkeys working happily, healthily, and accurately for 36 hours. Future breakthroughs may allow people to safely stay awake for several days straight. One group of researchers is studying a gene found in some fruit flies that lets them get by on one-third the usual amount of sleep. Another group is even working on an electric switch that instantly wakes up a sleeping brain.

The implications of this research are huge. On the one hand, this could lead to a world where we work longer and longer hours with less and less sleep. On the other hand, if we needed less sleep, we would have more free time to travel, read, volunteer, and spend time with family.

To sleep or not to sleep – that may soon be the question.

B Read the article again and answer the questions below.

1. What scientific research is mentioned in the article?
2. How much sleep does Norman Stanley think a person needs?
3. What ideas about the future are mentioned in the article?

C **Group work** Discuss these questions. Then share your answers with the class.

1. Do you think you get enough sleep?
2. What do you think would happen in the future if scientists found ways to let people stay awake longer? Would people be happier?

1. Types of people you might meet

starting point

A Read about six different types of people you sometimes meet on social occasions. Match the descriptions with the pictures.

1. It's a good idea to try out different topics to get a conversation going, and the **conversation starter** does just that. ____

2. Talking about your accomplishments too much is often considered rude, but that doesn't stop the **braggart**. ____

3. Saying nice things about others is customary for the **complimenter**. ____

4. It's rude to ignore your conversation partner, but the **wandering eye** does it anyway. ____

5. Talking about topics that interest you is fun. Unfortunately, the **bore** is interesting to no one else. ____

6. It's usually considered impolite to interrupt people, but the **interrupter** is always jumping into the conversation out of turn. ____

a — Excuse me, let me say . . .

b — Hi. Are you enjoying the party?

c — I really enjoyed . . .

d — I'm absolutely the best tennis player!

e — That's a great necktie!

f — So then I blah, blah, blah . . .

B **Pair work** Do you know any people like the six types above? What is it like to have a conversation with them?

"My best friend is kind of an interrupter. She's really nice, but I guess she just gets excited about the conversation and wants to jump in."

2 Infinitive and gerund phrases

grammar

It + be + adjective/noun + infinitive phrase is often used to comment on behavior.
These sentences can also be restated with gerund phrases.

It's rude to ignore your conversation partner.	**Ignoring** your conversation partner **is rude**.
It's a good idea to try out different topics.	**Trying out** different topics **is a good idea**.

The word *considered* may also follow *be* in this kind of sentence.

It's considered impolite to interrupt people.	**Interrupting** people **is considered impolite**.

These sentences can also include the phrase *for* + person/pronoun.

It's customary for the complimenter to say nice things about others.	**Saying** nice things about others **is customary for the complimenter**.

Grammar Plus: See page 114.

A Look at the starting point on page 36 again. Can you find more sentences that begin with gerunds? Try to change them into sentences beginning with *it's*.

B Rewrite the sentences using infinitive or gerund phrases. Then compare answers with a partner.

1. It's inappropriate to talk about politics at work or school.
   Talking about politics at work or school is inappropriate.
2. Using certain gestures is impolite in some foreign countries.
3. Asking someone's age is often considered rude.
4. It's not unusual in the U.S. to address a professor by his or her first name.
5. Hugging friends when you greet them is customary in many cultures.
6. Asking strangers if they're married is inappropriate in some countries.

3 What's appropriate?

vocabulary & speaking

A Are these words and phrases positive (+), negative (–), or neutral (~)?
Write the correct symbol next to each word.

___ 1. a compliment	___ 4. bad form	___ 7. offensive	___ 10. strange
___ 2. an insult	___ 5. inappropriate	___ 8. polite	___ 11. typical
___ 3. appropriate	___ 6. normal	___ 9. rude	___ 12. unusual

B **Group work** How do you feel about these things?
Discuss these situations using the words and phrases above.

1. You kiss people you meet on the cheek.
2. You and your classmates interrupt the teacher.
3. You stand very close to people when you talk to them.
4. You and your parents talk honestly and openly.
5. Your best friend calls you after 11:00 P.M.
6. You start a conversation with a stranger on a bus or subway.

"It's unusual for me to kiss people I meet on the cheek."

4 Making small talk

role play

A Small talk is light conversation with friends, acquaintances, or strangers. Check (✓) the topics that are appropriate for small talk.

What's Safe for SMALL Talk?

☐ Children and family   ☐ Health problems   ☐ Salaries

☐ Current affairs   ☐ Hobbies   ☐ Sports

☐ Entertainment   ☐ Marital status   ☐ The weather

B **Group work** Imagine you are at a party. Start a conversation, keep it going for one minute, and bring it to a close. Then find a new partner and repeat.

"Hi. How's it going?"

"Pretty good. Hey, did you see that soccer game last night?"

"I did! It's amazing to see our team play so well."

"I know! Hey, I should get going, but I'll call you later."

Useful expressions	
Conversation openers	**Conversation closers**
How's it going?	See you later.
Can you believe this weather? It's (awful)!	Sorry, I've got to run. Talk to you soon.
That's a great (jacket).	It was great to meet you.
Do you know many people here?	I should get going. I'll call you later.

5 Party talk

listening

A  Listen to three conversations at a party. Who is speaking in each one?

1. a. a mother and her son
   b. a teacher and her student
   c. a woman and her son's friend

2. a. two young students
   b. two older friends
   c. two co-workers

3. a. two cooks
   b. two wives
   c. two classmates

B Listen again. What closing phrase is used to end each conversation?

1. _____   2. _____   3. _____

 **Keeping a journal**

writing

> By expressing yourself in an English journal, you will become a better writer, learn to use new vocabulary, and improve your English.

A Read these journal entries from Eun Mi's family and a friend. How did each person react to her news? Write the correct letter.

___ annoyed   ___ pleased   ___ jealous

Yesterday morning, Eun Mi told us that she's decided to go to college in the United States next semester. A big argument broke out, mainly over the money. Studying abroad is so expensive, especially in the U.S.! Now everyone will have to work harder to pay for her expenses. It's irritating that she hasn't thought this through carefully.

Yesterday, Eun Mi said she's going to go to college in the United States. As she talked about it, I realized I was feeling upset. Ever since I can remember, I've wanted to study abroad. Now, if Mom and Dad spend the money to send Eun Mi abroad, I don't think they'll have any left to send me when I'm older. I know I should be happy for Eun Mi, but it's difficult to watch her always get everything she wants.

Yesterday, Eun Mi told me she's decided to go to college in the United States next semester to study fashion design. I've known Eun Mi nearly all my life, and I know this has always been her dream. I remember when we were just kids, Eun Mi used to talk about wanting to live in New York so she could get involved in the fashion world. It's wonderful to know that she'll be living out her dream in New York.

B What words or phrases helped you decide? Underline them. Then compare your answers with a partner.

C Imagine you have just received some important news. Write a journal entry expressing one of these reactions to the news.

- shock   - irritation   - delight   - fascination

D **Pair work** Exchange paragraphs with a partner. Then answer the questions.

1. What was your partner's reaction? Was it clearly stated?

2. What details can your partner include to improve this entry?

1. Eavesdroppers

starting point

A Read each person's statement. What do you think they should do about each situation?

I Wish I Hadn't Heard That!

Luis, 23, Mexico City

❝On the bus to work, I heard my boss's voice behind me. I think he was talking to the office manager on his cell phone. He was telling her that it would be a bad day at work. He explained that they were going to lay off my entire department!❞

Rebecca, 25, Vancouver

❝I overheard my roommate and her friend gossiping about me when I got home. I asked them what they were saying, but they claimed they hadn't been talking about me. I knew that wasn't true. It really hurt my feelings.❞

Hikari, 18, Nagoya

❝Last week, I overheard my little brother on his cell phone. He was warning his friend not to say anything. So of course I listened. He said he was getting a terrible grade in math this year! And he said it was a big secret too. In fact, my parents still don't know the truth.❞

B Group work Have you ever heard someone talking about you? What did you do?

2. Who can you confide in?

discussion

A Read the information in the chart. Would you rank each person in the same way?

Who do you tell first?

We asked a group of young adults to rate each person in the chart according to when they would tell that person different types of personal news (1 = tell first, 4 = tell last). This is what they said.

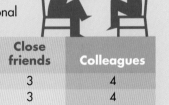

Who would you tell . . .	Family members	Spouses	Close friends	Colleagues
good news?	2	1	3	4
bad/tragic news?	1	2	3	4
gossip?	4	3	2	1
personal information?	3	2	1	4

Source: Interviews with people between the ages of 22 and 35

B Pair work Why would you tell something to one person and not to another? Discuss your reasons.

"I would usually talk about a personal problem with my close friends first because they already know most of my secrets."

3 Reported speech

Statements	Reported statements
"It's a big secret."	He said (that) it **was** a big secret.
"I'm getting a terrible grade."	He said (that) he **was getting** a terrible grade.
"They **got** engaged."	He said (that) they **had gotten** engaged.
"We **weren't talking** about you."	They claimed (that) they **hadn't been talking** about me.
"She**'s been** absent since Tuesday."	He said (that) she **had been** absent since Tuesday.
"We **had never been** there before."	She said (that) they **had never been** there before.
"I**'ll meet** you at the café."	He said (that) he **would meet** me at the café.

Questions	Reported questions
"**Did** you **know** about the layoffs?"	I asked him if he **had known** about the layoffs.
"What **are** you **saying**?"	I asked them what they **were saying**.

Commands	Reported commands
"**Don't say** anything!"	He warned his friend **not to say** anything.

General truths	Reported general truths
"The sun **rises** in the east."	She said (that) the sun **rises** in the east. (No change in tense.)

Grammar Plus: See page 115.

A Look at the starting point on page 40 again. Can you find more examples of reported speech?

B Rewrite the sentences using reported speech. Then compare answers with a partner.

1. "I'm not surprised at all."   She told me _____.
2. "Have you heard the news?"   He asked me _____.
3. "There's a bank down the street."   She said _____.
4. "Why aren't you talking?"   She asked me _____.
5. "Give him a call!"   He told me _____.
6. "We're getting married!"   She told me _____.
7. "Was the movie scary?"   The children asked me _____.
8. "We didn't take the 8:00 train."   They told me _____.

C **Pair work** Imagine that you have overheard this conversation. Take turns reporting each line of the conversation.

Ryan: I heard some interesting news today. Do you know Amanda Jenkins?

Lara: I know what she looks like, but I've never met her.

Ryan: Well, she's going to study for a year in Australia.

Lara: How can she afford that?

Ryan: She got a scholarship that will take care of all her expenses.

Lara: I think that's great. When is she leaving?

Ryan: I don't know . . .

"Ryan told Lara that he'd heard some interesting news today. He . . ."

4 Tell me what he said.

vocabulary & speaking

A Put these expressions for reported speech in the columns.

He claimed that . . .	He promised to . . .	He told me that . . .	He advised me to . . .
He asked me to . . .	He wanted to know . . .	He told me to . . .	He encouraged me to . . .
He warned me not to . . .	He explained that . . .	He asked me . . .	He wondered . . .

Statements	Commands or advice	Questions
He claimed that . . .		

B **Pair work** Tell a partner about a conversation you recently had. What was said? Use one of these topics or your own idea.

- an argument you had with a friend
- some exciting news a friend told you
- a time you asked someone for a big favor
- an apology you made or received

"My friend asked me if he could stay on my couch for a while. After a week, I told him . . ."

5 Tell me all about it!

listening

A Listen to Nicole's and Tony's news. Check (✔) the correct pictures.

I. Nicole

☐ **a.**   ☐ **b.**

2. Tony

☐ **a.**   ☐ **b.**

B Listen again. Circle the best answer to the questions.

1. Nicole's sister met her boyfriend . . .
   a. in the fall.
   b. yesterday.
   c. over four years ago.

2. Nicole's sister is probably . . .
   a. not afraid to be different.
   b. very traditional.
   c. shy.

3. How are things at the design studio?
   a. There isn't enough work.
   b. Things are picking up.
   c. Everything's about the same.

4. When will Tony's job end?
   a. In ten months.
   b. In less than a month.
   c. In the summer.

Mobile mania

reading

A Read the article. These headings are missing from the text. Put them in the correct place.

| The Generic Ring | The Distracted Driver | The Useless Call Maker |
| The I-Talk-Anywhere | The Shouter | The Corporate Big Shot |

Cell Phone Personality Types

In her travels, "Telephone Doctor" Nancy Friedman has noticed a variety of "cell phone personalities." Which of these types have you seen around?

1. The Shouter

Talking three times louder than necessary is characteristic of this offensive cell phone user. He seems to think everyone has a hearing impairment. Doesn't he know the phone already amplifies his voice?

2.

This pompous fellow makes all his business calls in public places while standing in the middle of a crowded room. He conducts big business deals right there in front of us, but we're not impressed.

3.

This exasperating person makes trivial phone calls, one after another, after another. On airplanes, you'll overhear her saying ridiculous things like, "*Hi, we haven't left yet,*" or "*Hi, we just landed. OK, see you in a minute.*"

4.

Making and taking calls anytime, anywhere is the trademark of this infuriating person. She'll chat in restaurants, at movie theaters, and even at funerals. When her cell phone rings, she looks at you and says insincerely, "*Oh, sorry about that.*"

5.

Drive or use the phone – don't do both at the same time. This can be dangerous. It's really scary to see a delivery truck in the rear view mirror with a distracted driver on a phone behind the wheel.

6.

These are the people who haven't bothered to personalize their ring tone. One phone rings and ten people check to see if it's theirs. Hang on, I think that's my phone!

Source: "What Type of Cell Phone User Are You?" by Nancy Friedman, www.telephonedoctor.com.

B Group work Does the article describe any cell phone users you know or have seen? What bad cell phone manners have you seen recently?

6 What's the real story?

1. Weird news

starting point

A Read the news articles. Match each headline with the correct article.

CELL PHONE
Opens Car Door

Sea Lion
Paints for Her Supper

Surfing Dog
Upstages Rivals

❶ The police have been called to a surfing contest in Brazil because a dog has been stealing all the attention. The dog became the main attraction at Praia da Tiririca

during the Surf World Championship. The dog and his owner surfed together on the same surfboard between the competitions. Police said, "They've called us to remove the pair because they've been getting more attention than the actual contest." The dog's owner said, "I've always surfed with my dog. He's always loved it. Sometimes I think he's a better surfer than I am!"

❸ A shopper in Michigan saved time and money after her husband helped her unlock her car – from 10 miles away. After a day at the mall, the woman went out to her car, but couldn't find her keys. When she saw them still in the ignition, she called home and said, "I've locked my keys in the car. I've never done that before. I don't know what to do." Following her husband's instructions, she held her cell phone about a foot from the car door, while her husband held the spare car remote near his phone and pressed the unlock button. The door unlocked. She said, "I've totally stopped worrying about my keys now."

❷ Maggie, a California sea lion at Pittsburgh Zoo, has been amazing visitors by painting for her supper. She has created dozens of paintings. Her trainer said, "I started teaching her to paint last year, and she caught on quickly." Maggie spent three months learning to hold the paint brush in her mouth and to touch it to the canvas. Adding the paint was the next step. Maggie earned a fish for every successful brush stroke. The trainer has saved all the paintings. She'll probably sell them to raise money to help animals.

B **Pair work** One of the news stories isn't true. Which one do you think it is? (For the answer, see page 152.)

> "I think story number one has got to be false. I just don't believe that a dog could surf.
> Story number two is also pretty amazing, but I have a feeling it's true."

2 Present perfect vs. simple past

grammar

Use the present perfect to report a recent event without giving a specific time reference.
The trainer **has saved** all the paintings.

Use the simple past to report an event with a specific time reference.
After a day at the mall, the woman **went out** to her car, but **couldn't** find her keys.
I **started** teaching her to paint **last year**.

Grammar Plus: See page 116.

A Look at the first story on page 44 again. Can you find more examples of the present perfect and the simple past? Why is each tense used?

B Complete the news story with the present perfect or past tense form of the verbs in parentheses. Then compare answers with a partner.

A group of thieves (1) *has stolen* (steal) the Dragon's Eye ruby from the Grand Gallery. Last night at about 1:00 A.M., the alarm (2) _____ (go) off. Police (3) _____ (rush) to the building immediately, but they (4) _____ (be) too late. Right after learning of the robbery, the mayor (5) _____ (set) up a telephone hotline for information about the theft. Three people (6) _____ (call) so far, but the police are still looking for further information. They believe it is probable that the thieves (7) _____ (left) the city. The curator of the Grand Gallery (8) _____ (offer) a $50,000 reward for information leading to the capture of the thieves.

3 Present perfect vs. present perfect continuous

grammar

Use the present perfect continuous to describe temporary situations and actions that are not yet completed. The present perfect describes permanent situations and recently completed actions.
A dog **has been stealing** all the attention. (temporary situation)
I've always **surfed** with my dog. (permanent situation)
Maggie **has been amazing** visitors by painting for her supper. (not yet completed action)
I've **locked** my keys in the car. (recently completed action)

Use the present perfect with the passive or with stative verbs such as *be*, *love*, and *have*.
He's always **loved** it.

Grammar Plus: See page 116.

A Look at the first story on page 44 again. Can you find another example of the present perfect continuous? Why is this tense used?

B Complete the sentences with the present perfect or present perfect continuous form of the verbs in parentheses. Then compare answers with a partner.

1. Many residents *have been* (be) homeless ever since last month's storm and _____ (stay) with relatives while their homes are being repaired.

2. Although crews _____ (repair) the subway signals all week, they still _____ (not solve) the problems with long delays.

3. Police _____ (guard) the stores that the thieves _____ (not rob) yet.

4. Workers _____ (plow) the roads all night, but some snow remains.

4. It's in the news.

vocabulary & speaking

A How would you define each of these news events?

epidemic	natural disaster	recession
famine	political crisis	robbery
hijacking	rebellion	scandal
kidnapping		

"A natural disaster is something like a volcano, an earthquake, or a flood."

B Pair work Tell your partner about some news stories you've recently heard. Use the words above.

"I saw something about a big scandal on the news this morning."

"Really? What was it?"

"Well, it said that a politician had been arrested for taking bribes."

5. Broadcast news

listening

A 💿 Listen to an early morning news broadcast. What is each story about? Write the correct number.

____ a natural disaster   ____ a scandal   ____ an unusual family   ____ an epidemic

B 💿 Listen again. Are the statements true or false? Check (✓) the correct answer. Then correct the false statements to make them true.

	True	False
1. TB is dangerous because it affects the heart.	☐	☐
2. One-third of all TB cases are untreatable.	☐	☐
3. The painting was bought by a wealthy person.	☐	☐
4. The painting may be a forgery.	☐	☐
5. Hurricane Pauline has trapped some people in their homes.	☐	☐
6. The tourist business in Cancún will be unaffected.	☐	☐
7. The mother left the house to give her children freedom.	☐	☐
8. The mother agreed to come down from the tree.	☐	☐

6. Speaking of the news

speaking

A Pair work Discuss the questions. Ask follow-up questions and add extra information.

1. How closely do you follow the news? What kind of stories interest you?

2. What do you think was the most important news story in the last few years?

3. Do you think stories about sports or celebrities count as "real news"?

B Group work Compare your answers with another pair. How are your opinions about the news different?

Narratives

writing

> A narrative is usually organized in chronological order and uses a variety of verb tenses.

A Number the events in this news story in the correct order. Then write a title for the article.

Title: _____

_____ As he was punching the shark, it began to release its grip on his leg.

_____ When the stunned shark finally let go, Anderson swam to shore, dragging his badly wounded leg behind him.

_____ He was pulling himself up on the rocks when another surfer came to his aid and called an ambulance.

_____ Anderson's leg was bleeding badly when emergency workers arrived, so they took him to a local hospital, where he was kept overnight for observation.

_____ In a post-Thanksgiving interview, Anderson said that even though he has had some bad dreams since the attack, he was looking forward to surfing again soon.

_____ Doctors released Anderson on Thanksgiving Day, and he was eating turkey at home with his family that afternoon.

__2__ Realizing it was a shark, he punched it repeatedly in the nose so it would loosen its grip.

__1__ Brian Anderson was surfing at a popular spot south of Seaside, Oregon, on the day before Thanksgiving when he noticed something was grabbing his leg.

_____ Anderson said he did this automatically because he'd heard on a TV show that sharks' noses are sensitive.

B Write a brief news story about a recent event. Use the simple past, present perfect, and present perfect continuous tenses to show the order of events.

C **Group work** Take turns reading your stories. Ask follow-up questions. Who has the most interesting story?

What happened?

starting point

A **Pair work** What do you think happened? Choose two stories. Complete them by filling in the gaps indicated by ◠◠▸.

1

certes / désormais / les emplois / selon / l'avenir

I went to the wrong class. It was the first day, so ◠◠▸. Afterwards, a classmate told me it was French IV and not my class, French I.

2

I'd picked up my mother's ring at the jeweler, but I couldn't find it when I got home. Up until then, I had never lost anything important, so I ◠◠▸. So, the ring wasn't lost after all! What a relief!

3

On my way home, I tried to take a shortcut through a neighbor's yard. As soon as I went through the gate, a huge dog suddenly ran up to me and ◠◠▸. Afterwards, we all laughed about it.

4

I had left for work a little earlier than usual. I got to the subway station, and ◠◠▸. When I got to work, my boss asked to speak to me. I knew he would never believe why I was late.

5

I volunteered to take care of my nephew. Before that, I'd never taken care of a toddler. As soon as his parents left, ◠◠▸. When they finally got home, the apartment, my nephew, and I were a mess!

6

Until my friends from Japan invited me to a sushi restaurant, I had never had sushi in my life. When I put the first piece in my mouth, ◠◠▸. They were really nice about it, though.

B **Group work** Take turns sharing your stories. Have you had similar experiences?

How did it all end?

listening

A Listen to two stories from the starting point. Which stories are they?

B Listen again. Choose the correct ending of each story.

1. a. He found the ring in his pocket.
   b. The jeweler had the ring.
   c. He bought a new ring.

2. a. The conductor helped her.
   b. A passenger helped her.
   c. The door finally opened.

3 Adverbs with the simple past and past perfect

grammar

Use these adverbs with the simple past to describe something that happens at a later time.
Afterwards, / **Later,** / **The next day,** we **laughed** about it.

Use these adverbs with the simple past to describe two things that happen at the same time.
When / **As soon as** / **The moment** I **got** to work, my boss **asked** to speak to me.

Use these adverbs with the past perfect to describe something that was true or that happened before another event in the past.
Up until then, / **Before that,** / **Until that time,** I **had** never **lost** anything important.

Grammar Plus: See page 117.

A Look at the starting point on page 48 again. Can you find the adverbs from the grammar box? Which verb tenses are used after them?

B Write two sentences for these situations using the adverbs from the grammar box. Then compare answers with a partner.

1. My apartment was robbed last week.

   Up until then, I had never had anything stolen. The moment it happened, I called the police.

2. I moved into my own apartment this summer.

3. I failed my driving test last week.

4. I really enjoyed my trip to Singapore last month.

5. I was nervous about going to the dentist.

6. I knew I shouldn't have agreed to give a short speech at my best friend's wedding.

C Match the sentences with the illustrations. Then compare answers with a partner.

__b__ 1. This morning, I was on my way to work.

____ 2. Last night, I was telling a joke at a dinner party.

____ 3. I was backing my car out of the garage. I crashed into my neighbor's car.

____ 4. I got to the punch line. I knocked a glass of water on the floor with my hand.

____ 5. She had never parked in front of my driveway.

____ 6. I noticed everyone laughed. I wasn't sure if they were laughing at the joke or at me.

D **Pair work** Take turns telling the stories for each picture. Use adverbs to show the order of events.

"This morning, I was on my way to work. I was backing my car out of the garage when I crashed into my neighbor's car. I couldn't believe it! Until then, she had . . ."

4 Embarrassing moments

listening

A 🔘 Listen to an interview with actor Tom Wiley. What jobs does he talk about?

1. _____ 2. _____ 3. _____

B 🔘 Listen again. Answer the questions.

1. Why did Tom lose his job at the department store?
2. Why didn't Tom last long as a painter?
3. Why was Tom fired from his job as a taxi driver?
4. How seriously do you think Tom took these jobs?

5 Creating a story

vocabulary & speaking

A These phrases are used to tell a story. Put them in the columns below.

I'll never forget the time . . .	Meanwhile . . .	To make a long story short . . .
The thing you have to know is . . .	And in the end . . .	I've got to tell you about . . .
It all started when . . .	That reminds me of when . . .	The other thing is . . .
What happened was . . .	The next thing we knew . . .	So finally . . .
I forgot to mention that . . .	So later on . . .	

Beginning a story	Continuing a story	Going back in a story	Ending a story
I'll never forget the time . . .			

B **Pair work** Tell a story about yourself. Use these story ideas and the phrases above. Ask follow-up questions.

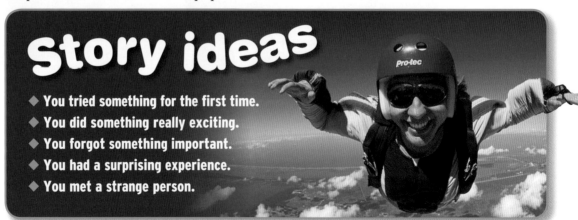

Story ideas

- ◆ You tried something for the first time.
- ◆ You did something really exciting.
- ◆ You forgot something important.
- ◆ You had a surprising experience.
- ◆ You met a strange person.

"I'll never forget the first time I cooked a big dinner by myself. I had always helped my mother cook, so I thought it would be easy."

"Why were you cooking a big dinner?"

"Well, I had invited all my friends over, and . . ."

C **Group work** Share your story with another pair of students. Then choose one of your group's stories and tell it to the whole class.

6 Personal anecdotes

A Pair work Look at the anecdote titles below. What do you think each one is about? Read the anecdotes to check your answers.

It happened to me!
(or my friend... or a friend of a friend...)

Baby-sitter's Blues

I'll never forget the time last winter when I was baby-sitting these two kids for the first time. It was about 7:30 at night. Their mom had asked me to make them a pizza for dinner. It had been in the oven for about fifteen minutes when suddenly I heard a noise outside, and the dog started barking. As soon as I opened the door and stepped outside, the kids slammed and locked it behind me. It was winter, and I stood outside freezing while they rolled around on the floor laughing hysterically. Meanwhile, the kitchen started getting smoky, and the smoke detector started buzzing. They didn't know what to do, so they let me back in. The pizza was burnt to a crisp.

I didn't say anything. But, as we sat around the kitchen table having a bowl of cold cereal instead of their favorite, pizza, I could tell they regretted what they'd done. Anyway, to make a long story short, I baby-sit them all the time now, and guess what? I haven't had any problems ever since that first night.

– AMY FERNANDEZ, BOSTON

A Bad Holiday

Have I learned any lessons the hard way? I sure have! What happened was I wanted a Monday off from work. Tuesday was a national holiday, and I thought a four-day weekend would be just perfect. I asked my boss, and he said no. At that company, all employees got their birthday off, so I asked if we could pretend that the Monday was my birthday. He said no. I woke up on the Monday morning feeling a little defiant, so I called in sick. I told them I got a terrible sunburn on the weekend. Later on, I realized that I had no color at all because I hadn't been out in the sun. So my friends and I went to the beach and stayed there all day. When I woke up the next morning, I had the worst sunburn of my life. I even had to go to the hospital! In the end, I learned a valuable lesson – I can't get away with anything!

– RITA WAGNER, SAN DIEGO

B Group work Discuss these questions. Then share your answers with the class.

1. Why do you think the baby-sitter hasn't had any more problems?
2. What would you have done if you were Rita?
3. Which story did you find the most amusing? Why?

C Group work Choose one of the topics below, or one of your own, and tell your group an anecdote. Who had the most interesting anecdote? Whose was the funniest?

- celebrity encounters
- childhood memories
- food experiences
- mistaken identity
- school days
- speaking English
- strange coincidences
- travel stories

Communication review

Self-assessment

How well can you do these things? Rate your ability from 1 to 5 (1 = low, 5 = high).

Talk about problems and solutions using time clauses (Ex. 1) _____

Talk about what someone has said using reported speech (Ex. 2) _____

Listen to a talk about stress (Ex. 3) _____

Give opinions about the best way to deal with stress (Ex. 3) _____

Tell anecdotes using simple past and past perfect (Ex. 4) _____

Now do the corresponding exercises below. Were your ratings correct?

 Calm down, chill out

speaking

A What do you do in these situations?

1. Tomorrow is a big day – you have a job interview or an exam. You are worried that you won't sleep well.

2. You've been lying in bed for hours and can't get to sleep. You can't stop thinking about what you have to do tomorrow.

3. You feel angry about something.

4. You are studying or working, and you need to take a break.

B Pair work Compare your answers with a partner. Are any of your solutions the same?

"Whenever I have something important the following day, I make sure I get some exercise so that I'll drop off as soon as I lie down."

2 **Guess what I heard?**

speaking

A Look at the situations below. Can you think of a personal example for each one?

1. You overheard someone say something really funny.

2. Someone told you a big secret.

3. You realized something important.

B Pair work Discuss your answers with a partner.

"I was on the subway, and I overheard this guy tell his friend that he'd gotten into the bathtub the night before and realized he was still wearing his socks! I just burst out laughing."

3. Stressed out!

listening & speaking

A  Listen to Andrew Philips talking about stress. What is the main topic of his talk? Check (✓) the correct answer.

☐ a. the stress of living on a tight budget

☐ b. college students and stress

☐ c. stress and nutrition

B Listen again. Check (✓) the causes of stress that you hear.

☐ 1. not having enough money   ☐ 3. noisy roommates   ☐ 5. not enough studying

☐ 2. part-time jobs   ☐ 4. too much studying   ☐ 6. not enough exercise

C **Pair work** Look at the causes of stress you checked above and these suggestions. Which do you think is the best way to deal with stress? Why?

Ways to Deal *with* Stress

▶ Find a physical activity you enjoy and make time for it.

▶ Organize your time.

▶ Make time to relax.

▶ Eat breakfast. Don't drink too much coffee.

▶ Develop a sense of humor.

"When you feel like you've got too much work, I think it's really important to sit down and organize your time. If you do, you'll feel more in control."

4. Tell me a story.

speaking

A **Pair work** Tell your partner about a time when one of these things happened to you.

- You met someone fascinating.
- You did something that took a lot of courage.
- Something made you laugh hysterically.

B **Group work** Join another pair and tell your stories. Ask and answer follow-up questions so that you will be able to retell each story.

"I once met a famous marathon runner at a café. It was pretty crowded, and I had just sat down at the last free table. The next thing I knew, she walked up and . . ."

The information age

LESSON A · A weird, wired world

1 Internet trends

starting point

A Look at these Internet trends. Check (✓) the ones that affect you.

← INTERNET TRENDS →

NOW . . .

☐ An increasing number of degrees are being offered online.

☐ Job openings have been advertised on the Internet for several years.

☐ Increasingly, news is being broadcast live on the Web.

☐ More music has been downloaded this year than ever before.

IN THE FUTURE . . .

☐ More computers will be infected by a new generation of dangerous viruses.

☐ An even greater variety of opinions will be posted on video blogs.

☐ More health-care sites are going to be used by people from home.

☐ The Internet is going to be used even more to download movies.

B **Pair work** What did people do before these trends appeared?

"People used to have to attend classes on campus to get a degree."

2 Technology buzzwords

vocabulary

A Match the Internet terms on the left with the definitions on the right.

1. download ___	a. software available for free
2. chat room ___	b. radio or TV shows for your MP3 player
3. hot spot ___	c. transfer files to your computer
4. blog ___	d. harmful software that attacks computers
5. freeware ___	e. short messages that are faster than e-mail
6. webcam ___	f. a place that has wireless Internet access
7. podcast ___	g. software that secretly records your online activity
8. spyware ___	h. a website where people have discussions
9. instant messaging ___	i. a camera that sends live video over the Internet
10. computer virus ___	j. an online journal of personal opinions

B **Pair work** Do you have any experience with these technologies?

"I've been downloading music and videos for years. And if I'm too busy to watch TV, I download podcasts of my favorite shows. It's great!"

3 Passive of present continuous, present perfect, future

grammar

Use these passive tenses for actions where the emphasis is on the object of the action.

Use the passive of the present continuous for ongoing actions.
An increasing number of degrees **are being offered** online.

Use the passive of the present perfect for recently completed actions.
More music **has been downloaded** this year than ever before.

Use *will* + passive or *be going to* + passive for actions that will begin in the future.
More computers **will be infected** by viruses.
More health-care sites **are going to be used** by people from home.   *Grammar Plus: See page 118.*

A Look at the starting point on page 54 again. Can you find one more example of each passive?

B Complete the sentences with the correct form of the verb in parentheses. Sometimes more than one answer is possible.

1. Thousands of computers already __have been infected__ (infect) by spyware.

2. More freeware _____ (released) soon for all kinds of applications.

3. Thousands of blogs _____ (start) on all sorts of topics every day.

4. Recently, more hot spots _____ (set up) in small towns.

5. Nowadays, teen chat rooms _____ (monitor) by concerned parents.

6. These days, podcasts _____ (downloaded) by people of all ages.

7. Soon viruses _____ (created) that no security software can detect.

8. Webcams _____ (used) in the future to broadcast college classes.

4 How do you feel about the Internet?

listening

A Listen to Edward, Ting, and Maria talking about how they use the Internet. Who do you think is the most enthusiastic about the Internet?

B Listen again. Does Edward (*E*), Ting (*T*), or Maria (*M*) mention these uses of the Internet? Write the correct letter.

____ 1. chat rooms   ____ 6. blogs

____ 2. news   ____ 7. e-mail

____ 3. webcams   ____ 8. instant messaging

____ 4. downloading   ____ 9. online courses

____ 5. computer games ____ 10. online shopping

5 Connecting ideas formally

vocabulary

A These expressions connect ideas in different ways. Put them in the columns below. Sometimes more than one answer is possible.

| additionally | for example | furthermore | in fact | nevertheless | similarly |
| as a result | for instance | indeed | likewise | on the other hand | therefore |

Add information	Compare or contrast	Emphasize	Give an example	Show result
additionally				

B Circle the appropriate connector to complete the sentences.

1. Tom loves technology; *similarly / for example*, he has the latest cell phone.

2. Many cities have wireless hot spots; *nevertheless / in fact*, others don't.

3. Most students do research online now; *nevertheless / therefore*, Internet access in libraries is a necessity.

4. Some websites aren't reliable; *as a result / likewise*, many people are being misinformed.

5. The Internet changes fast; *for example / likewise*, so do cell phones.

6. Blogs cover everything; *on the other hand / furthermore*, they are updated frequently.

6 Internet debate

discussion

A Pair work Do you think the Internet is a positive or negative influence? Find a partner who has the same opinion.

B Group work Find a pair who disagrees with you and your partner. Take turns explaining your reasons. Each pair gets a chance to disagree.

"The way I see it, the Internet is a positive influence because it brings us information from all over the world."

"That may be true, but in my opinion, that's not always a good thing. In fact, . . ."

Useful expressions		
Expressing opinions	**Disagreeing**	**Giving reasons**
If you ask me, . . .	That may be true, but . . .	That's why . . .
The way I see it, . . .	I see your point, but . . .	The reason for that is . . .

7 Writing a blog post

writing

> A blog, short for Web log, is an Internet journal or newsletter. Blogs are usually written about a specific topic, updated frequently, and intended for the general public to read.

A Look at the information about blogs. Then read the post below. Check (✓) the things this blog does or includes.

☐ 1. has a title or a headline   ☐ 4. provides links to other information

☐ 2. is written in a very formal style   ☐ 5. ends with a question

☐ 3. expresses a personal opinion

Weird Ideas

I was surfing the technology blogs this morning to see what unusual gadgets are out there these days. I found a blog that rated some new inventions. There sure is some weird stuff! I mean, they have these blankets with sleeves. You can sit in a chair with the blanket over you and hold a book or use your laptop and stay warm all over. I guess a few people might buy them. Maybe the same people who bought electric potato peelers. Then I started looking at the new electronic gadgets. That just got me depressed. It seems like gadget technology is changing so fast that if I buy the most up-to-date cell phone on the market, it'll be considered an old-fashioned clunker by the middle of next week. So here's my question: Is there even any point in trying to stay current?

2 comments

out-of-date cell phone

electric potato peeler

B Choose one of these topics or another of your own to write a short blog entry.

- celebrities
- games and gadgets
- online shopping
- sports
- cool websites
- international events
- parenting
- travel tips

C **Group work** Take turns reading your blogs and discuss these questions.

1. Whose entry is the most interesting or entertaining? Why?

2. What are some reasons why people write and read blogs?

3. Do you read blogs or would you like to read some? Which kinds?

Future shock

starting point

A Read these comments about technology. Do you agree or disagree?

What's YOUR take on technology?

Joo Chan, Seoul

"I get e-mail on my cell phone. That's nice, isn't it? Wouldn't it be great if everyone had a cell phone like that?"

Ana, São Paulo

"Isn't it weird how some people are always on their cell phones? They don't notice anything around them. It's actually dangerous, don't you think?"

Sarah, Los Angeles

"Don't you think there are too many websites? And most are full of misinformation. Shouldn't the government limit the number of sites?"

Yang-ming, Taipei

"Doesn't it seem like kids spend too much time in front of the TV? It makes them lazy, doesn't it?"

B **Pair work** Compare your answers with a partner. Do you think the government should regulate any of these things?

Forms of communication

vocabulary

A Where do you find these forms of communication? Put them in the columns below. Then add another expression to each category.

| banner ads | bus wraps | fliers | neon signs | spam | text-messaging |
| billboards | crawls | infomercials | pop-up ads | telemarketers | voice mail |

On television	On the Internet	On the telephone	On streets or highways

B **Pair work** Which of the above are the most useful ways of communicating information? The least useful? Do you find any of them annoying?

"Those crawls at the bottom of television screens aren't useful. It's impossible to read them and pay attention to a show at the same time. Don't you think they're annoying?"

3 Negative and tag questions for giving opinions

grammar

Use negative questions or tag questions to offer an opinion and invite someone to react.
Isn't it weird how some people are always on their cell phones?
Doesn't it seem like kids spend too much time in front of the TV?
Wouldn't it be great if everyone had a cell phone like that?
Shouldn't the government limit the number of sites?
I get e-mail on my cell phone. That's nice, **isn't it**?
TV makes kids lazy, **doesn't it**?

Use the phrase *don't you think* to form negative or tag questions.
Don't you think there are too many websites?
It's actually dangerous, **don't you think**?

Grammar Plus: See page 119.

A Look at the starting point on page 58 again. Find the two tag questions. Why do they have different endings?

B **Pair work** Turn the statements into negative or tag questions. Then ask and answer the questions. Discuss your answers.

1. It's sad how so many trees are being cut down to create junk mail.
2. They should get rid of those banner ads on the Internet.
3. It would be great if there were fewer billboards.
4. Teachers should ban text messaging during exams.
5. It's scary that opening a spam e-mail could expose your computer to a virus.
6. There are too many channels on TV these days.

4 It's kind of strange, isn't it?

discussion

A **Pair work** Do you agree or disagree with these opinions?

> Millions of people are addicted to the Internet these days. It's kind of strange, isn't it?

> Wouldn't it be great if they could eliminate all spam from e-mail?

> Don't you find it almost impossible to avoid pop-up ads?

> Shouldn't the government limit the types of websites allowed on the Internet?

> Don't you think a lot of people are being confused by misinformation on the Internet?

B **Group work** What problems are caused by modern information technology? Agree on the three most pressing problems and tell the class.

"Aren't kids today being exposed to too much information on television and the Internet? Won't they lose their ability to concentrate?"

"I don't think so. Don't you think kids today know more than previous generations?"

5 Health and technology

listening

A 🔘 Listen to a news report on technology. What is the report about? Check (✓) the correct answer.

☐ a. new high-tech medical treatments

☐ b. new health problems caused by technology

☐ c. vacation ideas for people who dislike technology

B 🔘 Listen again and complete the chart.

Problem	Symptoms	Treatment
eye strain		
carpal tunnel syndrome		
gadget addiction		

6 Gizmos and gadgets

discussion

A Read about these unusual gadgets. Would you like to have one? Why or why not?

The Gadgets of Tomorrow Are Here Today!

Never be away from the Internet again with Googler Goggles! These Internet glasses use the latest technology to allow you to enjoy 24/7 wireless Web access.

Finally, someone has invented a universal translator. Simply slip the Interpreter into your ear, set it to the target language, and you'll instantly understand every word being said.

You'll never be lost with the Global Positioning Helmet. It not only gives you directions to any place on earth, it also keeps track of your family and friends.

B **Group work** What new gadgets are becoming popular? Which ones do you like? What new gadgets do you think will come out in the future?

Cyber-begging

A Pair work Imagine that a stranger asked you for money to help pay off a frivolous debt. Would you help? Tell your partner. Then read the article.

Can you spare a dime for my *Gucci bills?*

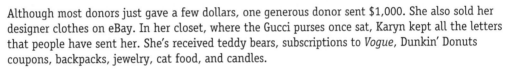

I
n June of 2002, Karyn Bosnak couldn't pay a $59.00 bill at the grocery store. She was officially broke. She didn't have enough money to get on the subway, but she looked rich. She was a television producer, earned $900 a week, and had a closetful of designer labels like Gucci and Louis Vuitton. But she also had a $20,221.40 credit card bill and an empty bank account. Karyn decided that it was time for a change. She built a website and simply asked people to help her out by sending her a buck or two.

On the site, Karyn honestly explained her situation, Gucci shoes and all. "If 20,000 people gave me just $1, I'd be home free, and I'm sure there are 20,000 people out there who can afford to give me $1." Amazingly, it worked. Her website was visited by more than a million people. She was on TV and in newspapers and magazines. She was offered a book deal and a movie contract. And of course, she was able to pay off her credit card debt.

Although most donors just gave a few dollars, one generous donor sent $1,000. She also sold her designer clothes on eBay. In her closet, where the Gucci purses once sat, Karyn kept all the letters that people have sent her. She's received teddy bears, subscriptions to *Vogue*, Dunkin' Donuts coupons, backpacks, jewelry, cat food, and candles.

It's hard to understand why so many people helped a total stranger pay off her huge credit card bill, but they did. Why? Karyn says, "I was just honest about what happened; I didn't make up some sob story about saving the world," she explains. Her donors think it's funny and original, she argues, and view it less as a charity than as an entertainment site.

Imitators have sprung up all over the Net, some with outrageously selfish requests like a BMW or a house. Actually, however, Karyn was not the first person to put up a website asking strangers for money. The practice has a name: "cyber-begging." Most sites receive little traffic and even less cash.

Karyn also had thousands of enemies and critics. People sent her hate mail and scolded her on websites. Karyn says she never let this anger bother her: "They are probably jealous they didn't think of it," she explains.

Source: "Brother, can you spare a dime for my Gucci bills?" by Janelle Brown, Salon.com

B Read the article again and answer the questions. Then compare your answers with a partner.

1. Why was Karyn in financial trouble in June 2002?
2. What was her main solution to her problem? What else did she do?
3. Why did so many people respond positively to her website?

C Group work Discuss these questions. Then share your answers with the class.

1. Do you think Karyn was unethical, or was she simply clever?
2. What would you have done if you were Karyn?

1 Creative professions

starting point

A **Pair work** How much creativity do these jobs require? Number them from 1 (most creative) to 4 (least creative). Explain your choices.

___ chef   ___ surgeon   ___ photographer   ___ jazz musician

"I think a chef has to be the most creative. Inventing new dishes requires a lot of creativity."

B **Group work** Which jobs might be right for these kinds of people? Discuss your answers.

1. someone able to think quickly
2. a person looking for adventure
3. people good with their hands
4. someone needing job security
5. a person trained in music
6. a person with a good voice

"Someone able to think quickly might be a good surgeon. You never know what might go wrong once the operation starts."

2 Creative qualities

vocabulary

A What qualities do creative people usually have? Complete the chart with the correct nouns or adjectives.

Noun	Adjective	Noun	Adjective	Noun	Adjective
curiosity	curious	innovation			passionate
decisiveness		knowledge		patience	
	determined		motivated	perceptiveness	
	disciplined		original		resourceful

B **Pair work** Which of the above qualities are most important to your job or studies? Discuss with a partner.

"Well, I'm studying engineering, and we get a lot of assignments, so I have to be very disciplined. It's a very competitive field."

3 Reduced relative clauses

grammar

You can shorten a relative clause by dropping the relative pronoun and the verb *be*.
Someone (**who / that is**) **able to think quickly** might be a good surgeon.
A person (**who / that is**) **looking for adventure** could be a private detective.
A person (**who / that is**) **trained in music** might be a good DJ.

You can also drop *who / that* and change the verb to the gerund.
Someone **who / that needs job security** might not want to be a jazz musician.
　　　needing job security

In many relative clauses, *who / that has* can be replaced by *with*.
A person **who / that has a good voice** could be a good TV journalist.
　　　with a good voice

Grammar Plus: See page 120.

A Look at the starting point on page 62 again. Can you make the reduced relative clauses in Exercise B into full clauses? What verb tenses do the full clauses use?

B Rewrite these sentences with reduced relative clauses. Then compare with a partner.

1. Someone who hopes to be a chef should get the proper training.
   Someone hoping to be a chef should get the proper training.
2. Anyone who wants to be an actor needs both talent and luck.
3. A person who works as a comedian is always looking for new ways to make people laugh.
4. People who are clever enough to get inside the mind of a criminal would make good detectives.
5. Anyone who dreams of becoming a champion athlete has to be prepared to do a lot of hard work.
6. Someone who is interested in the latest music trends might be a good DJ.
7. A person who is responsible for a large staff has to be able to be creative with scheduling.

C Complete these sentences using your own ideas.

1. . . . should keep up with current events.
   Anyone hoping to become a journalist should keep up with current events.
2. . . . should speak English as much as possible.
3. . . . needs to take voice lessons.
4. . . . doesn't need to have a good speaking voice.
5. . . . should follow the latest trends in clothing.
6. . . . has to study the behavior of animals.
7. . . . usually have a great love of food and eating.
8. . . . will find that the field is extremely competitive.

 **Creativity quiz**

discussion **A** How creative are you? Complete the quiz.

How CREATIVE Are You?

		Always	Sometimes	Rarely	Never
1.	Are you a risk taker?	3	2	1	0
2.	Are you naturally curious?	3	2	1	0
3.	Do you look for opportunities to improve things?	3	2	1	0
4.	Are you sensitive to beauty?	3	2	1	0
5.	Do you challenge accepted ideas?	3	2	1	0
6.	Do you keep an eye out for new fashions and products?	3	2	1	0
7.	Do you adapt easily to new situations?	3	2	1	0
8.	Do you trust your guesses, intuitions, and insights?	3	2	1	0
9.	Are you more interested in the future than in the past?	3	2	1	0
10.	Do you have a creative sense of humor?	3	2	1	0

B Add up your score. Then check what your score means below. Do you agree?
Tell your partner.

About You	**21–30**	**11–20**	**0–10**
	Because you're open-minded, you like to keep up with the latest trends and innovations. Accepting the status quo bores you. You see mistakes as learning experiences.	You often have good ideas, but you prefer to feel them out with friends before taking action. You're up-to-date with new fashions and products, but unlikely to be the first in your group to try them.	You prefer to stick with the tried-and-true, which helps you feel safe, but you may get left behind in later years. You're content with who you are and what you know.

 Creativity at work

listening **A** 🔘 Listen to Samira, Alex, and Naomi talking about their occupations.
What does each person do?

B 🔘 Listen again. Does Samira (*S*), Alex (*A*), or Naomi (*N*) do these things?
Write the correct letter.

    ____ 1. stay on top of trends   ____ 4. help clients decide what looks best

    ____ 2. answer the phones   ____ 5. think about the competition

    ____ 3. work long hours   ____ 6. present ideas to clients

6. Beginning new paragraphs

writing

> Begin a new paragraph each time you change the focus of your ideas.

A Read this composition and decide where the writer changes focus. Write a (P) where two new paragraphs should begin. Then compare answers with a partner.

Lucy Gomez is the most creative person I know. She started piano lessons when she was only 6 years old. At school, she was always creating interesting projects in her art class. When she was only 12 years old, she won a citywide poetry contest. Her parents were very proud of her. Lucy works as a sitcom writer for a popular TV show now. She works with a group of writers, and together they have to think of original ideas for stories. They also have to come up with funny dialogue for the actors on their show, because the actors have to play believable characters that will make the audience laugh. It is not an easy job, but Lucy does it well. She starts work late in the morning and often works until 7 or 8 at night. Lucy is very curious. She likes to travel and meet new people who have opinions that are different from hers. She usually carries a notebook with her and writes down what she sees and hears. She tells me that these new experiences are a good source of ideas for her work. I always enjoy talking to her and am happy to know someone as knowledgeable and creative as Lucy.

B Brainstorm ideas for a composition about someone who is very creative or who is unique or different in an interesting way. Answer these questions to help you.

1. In what ways is this person special or different?
2. How does this affect his or her life?
3. Would you like to be like this person? Why or why not?

C Write a three-paragraph composition based on your ideas.

D **Pair work** Read your partner's composition and answer these questions.

1. Are the paragraphs divided where they should be?
2. Is the focus of each paragraph clear?
3. Is there any additional information that you would like to know that was not included?

1. Everyday objects

A Read about these unusual uses of everyday objects. Have you ever used them in these ways?

Three Clever Ideas

1 "I have three cats, which means there's usually a lot of cat fur on my clothes. To get rid of the fur, I wrap my hand in tape, sticky side out. Then I rub the tape over my clothes, and it picks up the fur!"

2 "The zipper was stuck on my favorite jacket. Luckily, my roommate works in fashion, which is great because she knew how to fix it. She just rubbed a drop of olive oil on the zipper."

3 "I put my entire CD collection on my MP3 player, so now I have all these useless discs lying around. I hate throwing things away, which is why I use them as beverage coasters."

B **Group work** Now use your imagination to suggest uses for these everyday items. Decide on the best use for each and share it with the class.

- old newspapers
- a shower curtain
- clothespins
- empty shoe boxes
- dental floss
- safety pins
- empty jars or cans
- rubber bands

"You can put old newspapers in the bottom of a bird cage so it's easier to clean."

2. Exploring possibilities

vocabulary & speaking

A Combine the verbs with the nouns to make common expressions.

Verbs			Nouns			
analyze	find	organize	a mistake	a situation	alternatives	information
explore	make	solve	a problem	a solution	possibilities	

analyze a situation, solve a problem . . .

B **Pair work** Discuss the questions. Then ask your partner more questions using the new vocabulary.

1. When you make decisions, do you explore all the possibilities first?
2. Who do you talk to when you need to find a solution to an important problem?
3. When was the last time you analyzed a mistake you made? What did you learn from it?

3 Non-defining relative clauses as sentence modifiers

grammar

You can use non-defining relative clauses with *which* to make a comment about an entire sentence.

I have three cats, **which means there's usually a lot of cat fur on my clothes**.

My roommate is a slob, **which is why I want to get my own apartment**.

Grammar Plus: See page 121.

A Look at the starting point on page 66 again. Find more examples of these grammar patterns and notice how commas are used.

B Match these statements with the appropriate non-defining clauses. Then compare with a partner and write two similar statements of your own.

1. I want to give away all my old books, __h__

2. I had locked my keys in my car, ____

3. I'm going to repaint my room next week, ____

4. My son made a robot costume for himself, ____

5. Our neighbor saves her empty jars for my dad, ____

6. My new cell phone can store and play music, ____

7. It's easy to get lost when driving in a new city, ____

8. Adam still listens to music on an old-fashioned record player, ____

a. which is why you saw me opening it with a coat hanger.

b. which is great since he uses them to store nails and things in his workroom.

c. which is great because I can listen to it while I'm on the subway.

d. which is why I've been saving old newspapers.

e. which is why personal navigation systems were developed for cars.

f. which is why he was covered in aluminum foil yesterday.

g. which is strange since cassettes and CDs have been around for so long now.

h. which means I have to get boxes for them.

4 Key inventions

speaking

A What inventions or discoveries do you think have had the greatest impact on modern life? Make a list.

the cell phone

the television

the airplane

B **Group work** Compare lists with your group.

"I think the cell phone has really changed our lives. People can talk wherever they are, which means they can always be in touch and save time."

5 Great ideas

listening

A Look at the pictures. What do you know about these products or services? How do you think they were developed?

B 💿 Listen to these stories about the invention and development of the products above. Complete the chart.

	Bill Bowerman	Fred Smith
How they got the idea		
The initial reaction to the idea		
What the inventors did in response		

6 Making life better

discussion

A **Pair work** Why do people create or invent new products? Read this list of reasons and add two more of your own.

- to help protect people's health
- to make business more efficient
- to make daily life easier
- to make life more enjoyable

- to protect the environment
- to save lives
- _____
- _____

B **Group work** Join another pair. Why do you think these things were created or invented? Use the reasons in Exercise A or others of your own.

1. air conditioners
2. artificial sweeteners
3. digital cameras
4. electric knives
5. handheld computers
6. hybrid cars
7. karaoke machines
8. lie detectors
9. MP3 players

"Air conditioners were invented to protect people's health. The summer heat can be deadly for infants and the elderly."

7 Modern inventions

A Read the title of the article. What modern machine do you think Daisuke Inoue invented? Then read the article and check your answer.

The Man Who Taught the World to Sing

Daisuke Inoue was a drummer in a band near Osaka, Japan, that played versions of famous pop songs. People loved to sing along as the band played, but most of them couldn't carry a tune. Inoue's band had spent years learning how to make the untalented customer sound in tune by adjusting the music to match the customer's voice. The singers, mainly Japanese businessmen out for a night on the town, loved Inoue's unique follow-along style.

In 1971, a loyal client asked Inoue to escort him on a company trip, but Inoue could not attend. He found a solution: he recorded his band's back-up tracks, and then hooked up a car stereo and an amplifier. With this device, Inoue gave birth to the karaoke machine. By the 1980s, *karaoke*, which means "empty orchestra," was a Japanese word that required no translation across the globe.

Unfortunately, Inoue never bothered to patent the world's first karaoke machine, so he lost his chance to become one of Japan's richest men. When asked if he regretted not patenting his invention, 65-year old Daisuke Inoue confessed, "I'm not an inventor. I am just resourceful. I simply put things that already exist together. Who would consider patenting something like that?"

Although Inoue spent years in obscurity, in 1999, *Time* magazine called him one of the 20th century's most influential people, saying he had "helped to liberate the once unvoiced."

Inoue is always getting asked silly questions, but he takes them in stride. "Women approach me all the time and ask if I can help their husbands sing better. I always say that if her husband were any good at singing, he would be making a living at it. He's bad, which means he's just like the rest of us."

Inoue's friend Robert Scott Field says, "Some people say he lost 150 million dollars. If it were me, I'd be crying in the corner, but he's a happy guy. I think he's amazed to find that he's touched so many lives." Inoue believes the little box he put together has had a huge social impact, especially in Japan. At weddings and company get-togethers, the karaoke comes out and people relax. It breaks the ice.

Daisuke Inoue is also the subject of a movie about his life, called simply, *Karaoke*. The film was released in Japan and starred a good-looking actor. "At least they got someone tall to play me," Inoue laughs.

Inoue didn't use a modern karaoke machine until he was 59 years old, but his favorite English songs are "Love Is a Many Splendored Thing" and Ray Charles' "I Can't Stop Loving You." "They're easy, which is good because I'm a terrible singer," said Daisuke Inoue, the man who taught the world to sing.

Source: "Mr. Song and Dance Man," by Dr. David McNeill, Sophia University, Tokyo

B **Group work** Discuss these questions. Then share your answers with the class.

1. Do you think Daisuke Inoue should receive compensation for his invention? Explain.

2. Would you have the same attitude as Inoue if you invented something popular and received no compensation? Why or why not?

3. Why do you think karaoke has become so popular around the world?

9 Generally speaking

LESSON A · How typical are you?

1. What's typical?

starting point

A Read about the "typical" person in Italy and Japan. What information surprised you?

The typical **Italian** person...	The typical **Japanese** person...
drinks **155 liters** of bottled water per year.	drinks **10 liters** of bottled water per year.
consumes **3.2 kilograms** of coffee per year.	consumes **0.9 kilograms** of coffee per year.
consumes **0.1 kilograms** of tea per year.	consumes **0.9 kilograms** of tea per year.
visits the doctor **6 times** per year.	visits the doctor **14 times** per year.
watches **27 hours** of TV per week.	watches **32 hours** of TV per week.
gets married at **30 years old** (for men) or **27 years old** (for women).	gets married at **30 years old** (for men) or **27 years old** (for women).
drives on the **right side** of the road.	drives on the **left side** of the road.
finds school boring.	**doesn't find** school boring.

Source: www.nationmaster.com

B Complete these statements. Use information from the chart above.

1. While the typical _____ finds school boring, the typical _____ doesn't.
2. Unlike the Japanese, Italians seem to drink a lot of _____.
3. Both like TV, except that the typical _____ watches more of it.
4. In contrast to Italian drivers, Japanese people drive on the _____.
5. Both groups are fairly different, except for the age _____.

2. That's just so typical!

speaking

A **Pair work** What are typical examples of these things in your hometown?

1. a pet   2. a home   3. a job   4. a car   5. a snack food   6. a weekend activity

B **Group work** Join another pair and compare your answers.

"What's a typical pet in your hometown?"

"People mostly have dogs. For the most part, they're small dogs because the apartments in my city aren't too big."

3 Clauses and phrases showing contrast and exception

grammar

Use *while*, *unlike*, and *in contrast to* in order to present contrasting information, especially in writing.
While the typical Italian person thinks school is boring, the typical Japanese person doesn't.
Unlike the Japanese, Italians seem to drink a lot of bottled water.
In contrast to Italian drivers, Japanese people drive on the left.

Use *except (that)*, *except (for)*, and *except for the fact (that)* to show an exception.
Both like TV, **except (that)** the typical Japanese person watches more of it.
Italian and Japanese people are fairly different, **except for** the age they get married.
Japanese people typically consume less, **except for the fact that** they drink more tea.

Grammar Plus: See page 122.

A Look at the starting point on page 70 again. Notice the sentences that use phrases with *except*. Which phrase is followed by a clause?

B Here's some information about customs. How are they different in other places? Write sentences showing contrasts and indicating exceptions.

1. When people in the U.S. go to a party, they usually arrive a few minutes late.
   Unlike people in the U.S., most people where I live arrive on time for parties.
2. Most people in Canada have cereal and milk for breakfast.
3. Most people in Korea who study a foreign language choose English.
4. In the U.K., it's common for friends to split the bill at a restaurant.
5. For people in Italy, lunch is the main meal of the day.
6. Women in Spain usually kiss people on both cheeks when they meet.

C Are you typical? Complete these sentences and compare with a partner.

1. Unlike most *men* / *women* where I live, *I don't wear makeup.*
2. In contrast to most of my friends, . . .
3. While a lot of the people where I live . . .
4. I'm similar to many of my friends, except that . . .

4 Typical student profile

discussion

Group work Complete this profile. Then compare answers with your group.

Are you typical?

☐ **1.** I have never shopped online.
☐ **2.** I eat breakfast every morning.
☐ **3.** I have a full- or part-time job.
☐ **4.** I have visited a foreign country.
☐ **5.** I use public transportation.
☐ **6.** I keep a daily personal diary.

"Unlike most people in the class, I've never shopped online. I don't want a hacker to get my credit card information."

5 Should I just go with the flow?

vocabulary

A Are these adjectives, verbs, and phrases related to accepting things as they are or to making changes? Put them in the columns below.

Adjectives	Verbs	Phrases
amenable	accept	be your own person
conservative	conform (to)	challenge the status quo
nonconformist	confront	fit in
rebellious	rebel (against)	follow the crowd
unconventional	stand up (to/for)	make waves

Accepting things as they are	Making changes

B **Group work** Use the expressions above to describe three famous people from the past or present. Give reasons for your answers.

"Someone who has made great changes in the world is Nelson Mandela. He wasn't afraid to challenge the status quo. He stood up for his beliefs and was even willing to go to jail."

6 How are they different?

listening & speaking

A 🔘 Listen to Yoshiko, Renato, and Suzanne talking about their school experiences. Answer the questions.

1. What examples does Yoshiko give for how she is typical? In what way is she different?

2. What are three ways that Renato's life is typical? What does he like to do that makes him different?

3. Does Suzanne give an example of how she is different? If so, what is it?

B 🔘 Listen again. Do you think Yoshiko, Renato, and Suzanne believe they are more typical or different from most people their age?

C **Pair work** Do you tend to go with the flow or be your own person? Discuss these questions.

1. How do you feel about changing jobs or schools?

2. Do you try to have a unique look in clothes?

3. Do you like mainstream music?

4. Do you ever change your routine just because you're bored?

Yoshiko in Mexico

7 Supporting statements

writing

> Supporting statements develop the topic sentence by providing key facts, reasons, or examples.

A Read the paragraph and underline the topic sentence and three supporting statements that develop the main idea. Then compare your answers with a partner.

My Blog

http://www.cup.org/myblog/

My friend Josie . . .

June 13

My friend Josie doesn't like to follow the crowd. While most of us are trying our best to fit in with everyone else, Josie likes to be her own person. For instance, she has her own unique sense of fashion, so she likes to buy all her clothes, except for her shoes, in used clothing shops. Her taste in music is also pretty unconventional. Unlike most of my friends, she can't stand pop music. She prefers to listen to Philippine and Andean folk music. She also has a very interesting job. Unlike her old nine-to-five job in a conservative department store, she now works as a trendspotter for an advertising company. This means that she spends her time looking at the latest fashion and entertainment trends among young people. Then she writes reports for her company about what's in style.

[4 comments]

B Finish these statements with information of your own to make topic sentences. Compare with a partner.

1. Generally speaking, most people where I live don't . . .
2. One of my best friends is . . .
3. In general, my friends tend to be . . .

C Choose one of the topic sentences above and brainstorm supporting ideas. Then choose at least four supporting statements and write a paragraph.

Generally speaking, most people where I live don't mind challenging the status quo. It's their way of . . .

D **Pair work** Exchange paragraphs and answer these questions.

1. Do all the supporting statements relate to the topic sentence?
2. Do they develop and explain the topic sentence?
3. Do the supporting details fit together in a logical order?
4. What other points or examples could be added?

Student concerns

starting point

A Read Annie's e-mail to her friend. What problems does she have?

To: Adriana da Costa
From: Annie Wilson
Subject: Missing you!

Hi Adriana,

How are things back in Rome? Are you glad to be home again? Sorry I haven't written lately. I've been a bit depressed. My grades aren't as good as they used to be. Classes didn't use to be so difficult!

I have to say, I miss you. You used to be such a good influence on me! These days, I oversleep. I often miss my classes! That never used to happen because I knew I had to meet you at the café in the morning. I remember how you would complain about the coffee here in Canada. You used to call it "brown water"!

I'm spending too much money too. Every time I go to the mall, I see something I want to buy. That's another reason I miss you! I would see some great jacket, but you wouldn't let me buy it. You would always tell me I didn't need it and drag me away!

Also, I have a noisy new roommate, Cindy. All she ever does is gab on her cell! Remember the way we would sit around talking? You always used to make me laugh. I bet that's a big reason I never used to feel stressed like I do now!

Anyway, exams will be over on Friday, so I'm sure I'll feel better then.

Write soon!
Annie

B **Pair work** What do you think Annie should do about her problems?

"Annie should buy a second alarm clock so she won't miss class."

Expressions with *keep* and *stay*

vocabulary

A Match the phrases to make questions. Notice the expressions with *keep* and *stay*.

1. When friends move away, do you **keep / stay** _c_   a. their grades up?
2. When you're stressed, can you **keep** ___   b. up with a class?
3. After studying all night, how do you **stay** ___   c. connected?
4. Do you ask for help if it's hard to **keep** ___   d. in touch?
5. Do you break the rules or do you **keep / stay** ___   e. things in perspective?
6. What can students do to **keep** ___   f. awake in class?
7. Is it important for old friends to **keep / stay** ___   g. out of trouble?

B **Pair work** Take turns answering the questions. Discuss your answers.

3 Past habitual with *used to* and *would*

grammar

Used to and *would* can both be used to describe past actions or situations which are no longer true. However, *would* cannot be used with stative verbs such as *live*, *be*, *have*, or *like*.

You always **used to make** me laugh.
Classes **didn't use to be** so difficult.
Remember the way we **would sit** around talking?
I **would** see some great jacket, but you **wouldn't let** me buy it.

Grammar Plus: See page 123.

A Look at the starting point on page 74 again. Make a list of the things that have changed for Annie since Adriana went back to Italy.

B Complete these sentences with *used to* or *would*. Sometimes more than one answer is possible.

The first year of high school, I wasn't a very good student. I (1) _____used to_____ think school was boring. I remember my classmates (2) _____ go to the library and work on projects or study, but I (3) _____ go to the video arcade instead. I (4) _____ go right after class and (5) _____ spend about two hours there. I knew I was smart, so I wasn't worried about my grades. My mom (6) _____ have a job, so she never knew what time I (7) _____ get home. One day, I had to go to the principal's office. He said, "You (8) _____ be a great student. Now your grades are terrible. Explain!" That was a real wake-up call. After that, I (9) _____ be at the library most nights with my classmates. Now that my kids are in high school, I tell them about all the silly things I (10) _____ do when I was their age.

4 Personal concerns

discussion

A **Pair work** These people have had a change in their lives. What positive or negative impacts have these changes had?

Britney Majors
32, Toronto

"Before my promotion, my colleagues and I would eat lunch together. Now they seem uncomfortable around me. But with my new salary, soon I'll be able to afford a new car."

Luis Santos
25, São Paulo

"Before my wife and I had our first baby, we would go out whenever we wanted. We can't do that now. I didn't use to be a worrier, but I am now."

Wen-ho Chen
63, Taipei

"We used to plan on moving in with our son when we retired. But we've changed our minds. We just sold our house, and we're going to travel the world."

B **Group work** Think about a big change in your life. Talk about the positive and negative impacts it had.

"Last year, I was transferred to another department in my company. My new responsibilities are a lot more interesting, but I didn't use to have to work this much."

5 Different approaches to problem solving

listening & speaking

A **Pair work** Read about these three approaches to problem solving. What method do you use? Give examples to support your answer.

What kind of problem solver are you?

Different people solve their problems in different ways. The three main approaches are assertive, meditative, and cooperative. Find out which one best describes you.

◆ **Assertive** people prefer action to talk. When they're faced with a problem, they immediately try to work out a solution.

◆ When **meditative** people have a problem, they sit and think about it, and might even do research. Sometimes, the answer comes to them if they don't act on something right away.

◆ **Cooperative** people think the easiest way to solve a difficult problem is to ask for help. Another person's perspective can help cooperative people come up with solutions.

"I'd say I'm a meditative person. Before I bought my first car, I spent hours doing research on it by myself. It took me forever to decide!"

B Listen to Dominique, Carla, and Wayne talking about their personal concerns. What kind of problem solver is each person?

C Listen again. What are two things each person did to solve their problem?

6 Here's an idea . . .

role play

A Read about these people's problems. What advice would you give each person?

> My boss is so demanding. She gives me more work than I can handle.

> I can't save money because I always spend it on little things I want but don't really need.

> My last job interview went very badly. I always get tongue-tied in front of authority figures.

> I studied for years to do my current job. But now I'm not sure I really want this career.

B Role-play each situation. Take turns giving and receiving advice.

"My boss is so demanding. She gives me more work than I can handle."

"Here's an idea. See if your co-workers feel the same way. Maybe you all can talk to the boss about it."

"I guess I could try that."

7. Good advice

A **Pair work** Do you give your friends good advice? Discuss with a partner. Then read the article.

Are We **Advice** Junkies?

Picture the following scenario:

Your best friend is spending a lot of time with a neighbor of hers, someone you really don't like. You're convinced this person is a bad influence. One night, your friend calls you and asks you for your opinon.

You tell your friend precisely what you think of her neighbor and suggest she avoid this person. The next week, you spot your best friend and her neighbor walking down the street and laughing, and although you feel hurt, you know why your friend's been avoiding you.

While this situation isn't unusual, the damage arises because almost no one can resist the temptation to speak his or her mind. We are so addicted to giving advice by telling friends what they should do, that we don't give them the opportunity to work through a crisis by themselves. All they want is for us to be their sounding board so we can allow them to explore their feelings.

When we give friends our resolutions to their dilemmas, we make them feel accountable if they don't follow our advice, and we create an occasion for them to play the "yes, but" game, so their problem becomes our problem.

How do we give competent and effective counsel to our friends when they're in a quandary? Here are a few pointers:

- Don't take responsibility for your friends' troubles. Be there, but don't try to take over and decipher the problem for them.

- Don't be judgmental. Try not to create guilt by passing on your own opinions and standards.

- Reflect their feelings as they talk. Say, "I can see this is frustrating for you."

- Ask open-ended questions in contrast to yes or no questions. "How did you feel when your mother visited last week?"

- Remember, if we always allowed our friends to use us as their main source of comfort and consolation, it would prevent them from taking responsibility for their own problems.

Source: "Have you become the local wailing wall?" by Susan Erasmus, www.health24.com

B **Role play** Work with a partner. Take turns being the listener and practice using the skills outlined in the article. Use these situations or your own ideas.

- Your classmate calls to complain about failing an important exam.
- Your cousin grumbles about not having enough money.
- Your friend is having a problem with one of her colleagues.

Self-assessment

How well can you do these things? Rate your ability from 1 to 5 (1 = low, 5 = high).

Talk about trends with verbs in the passive (Ex. 1)   _____
Talk about changes in people's lifestyles with *used to* and *would* (Ex. 1)   _____
Make predictions with future forms of the passive (Ex. 2)   _____
Listen and talk about character traits using reduced relative clauses (Ex. 3)   _____
Discuss "typical" behavior with clauses showing contrast and exception (Ex. 4)   _____

Now do the corresponding exercises below. Were your ratings correct?

 How things have changed!

discussion

A Think about how information technology has changed in the past few years. How have people's shopping habits, hobbies, and social lives been affected?

B **Pair work** Compare your answers with a partner.

"I think people used to be really nervous and would think twice about buying anything online. Now that more secure systems are being used, it's a lot safer, and online shopping is a lot more popular."

"Yeah, I think so too. Most people have been convinced that it's safe. Even my grandmother buys and sells stamps online!"

 What next?

discussion

A **Pair work** What do you think will happen in the next ten years as a result of new technologies in these areas?

1. communication   4. finance
2. education   5. medicine
3. entertainment   6. sports

B **Group work** Compare your predictions in groups.

"Ten years from now, I think music will be sold only on the Internet. What do you think?"

3 Team roles: The perfect "STEAM" team

listening & speaking

A Listen to the phone conversation between Tony and Annie. What was special about the day? Check (✓) the correct answer.

☐ a. Tony was chosen for the football team.

☐ b. Annie thinks Tony is creative.

☐ c. It was Tony's first day at work.

B Listen again. Match the roles on the left with the personality types on the right.

Role	Personality type
1. Solver _ᴅ_	a. disciplined
2. Team manager ____	b. patient
3. Explorer ____	c. passionate
4. Analyst ____	d. creative
5. Motivator ____	e. resourceful

C **Pair work** Look at the roles above. Which role do you think you would be best at or would enjoy the most? Why? Compare your ideas with a partner.

"I think I'd probably be best in an Explorer role. I'm pretty resourceful. What about you?"

"I'm a person with a lot of patience, but I'm not that creative. I'm more of a Team manager type."

4 That's so typical!

speaking

A Complete this chart with your opinions about typical parents and teenagers.

	The typical parent	The typical teenager
What are some of their concerns?		
What is their most valued possession?		
How much time do they spend with friends?		
What do they use the Internet for?		
What do they like to do on vacation?		

B Write at least four sentences contrasting the typical parent with the typical teenager. Then compare with a partner.

"Generally, the typical teenager is concerned about friends, while the typical parent is concerned about their children."

10 The art of complaining

1. Everyday annoyances

starting point

A Have you ever had a problem similar to these? Do you agree or disagree with these comments?

"The thing that I hate is when kids ride their scooters on the sidewalk."

"One thing that bothers me is when my friends don't show up on time for things."

"Something that bugs me is people who take up two seats on a crowded bus."

"The thing I can't stand is co-workers who leave their cell phones ringing on their desks."

B **Group work** Look at the situations above. Would you complain, or would you be quietly annoyed?

2. It really irks me!

listening & speaking

A Listen to Jane and Kyle talking about irritating situations. What is bothering each person?

B Listen again. Discuss the questions.

1. Whose situation do you think was more annoying, Jane's or Kyle's?

2. Who do you think handled the situation better, Jane or Kyle?

3. How would you have reacted in each situation?

3 Relative clauses and noun clauses

grammar

A relative clause can occur in the subject or the object of a sentence.
Something **that bugs me** is people **who take up two seats on a crowded bus**.
The thing **(that) I can't stand** is co-workers **who / that leave their cell phones ringing on their desks**.

Some sentences use a relative clause and a noun clause beginning with a question word such as *when*.
The thing **(that) I hate** is **when kids ride their scooters on the sidewalk**.
One thing **that bothers me** is **when my friends don't show up on time for things**.

Grammar Plus: See page 124.

A Look at the starting point on page 80 again. Which clauses are relative clauses? Which are noun clauses?

B **Pair work** Complete the sentences with your own opinions. Then discuss them with a partner.

1. Something that bothers me about my friends is . . .
   when they don't return my calls.
2. One thing that irks me about my neighbors is . . .
3. If I'm riding in a car, something that irritates me is . . .
4. The thing that aggravates me most is a friend . . .
5. The thing that annoys me about people talking on cell phones is . . .
6. . . . is one thing that bothers me at home.

4 That drives me up the wall!

vocabulary

A Combine the verbs with the phrases. How many combinations can you make? How are their meanings different?

Verbs	Phrases		
drive	on someone's nerves	someone mad	someone's blood boil
get	someone crazy	someone sick	someone's goat
make	someone down	someone up the wall	under someone's skin

B **Group work** How do these things make you feel? Discuss these situations using the expressions above.

1. people laughing at their own jokes
2. vending machines that "steal" your money
3. finding empty ice cube trays in the freezer
4. people eating on public transportation
5. airlines not serving food on long flights

"The thing I hate is when people laugh at their own jokes and they're not funny!"

5 Polite complaints

discussion

A Which of these descriptions fits you best? Give examples to support your answer.

"I very rarely complain."   *"I only complain if I absolutely have to."*   *"I complain because it's my right."*   *"I complain about every little thing."*

a silent sufferer   **a calm, collected type**   **an activist**   **a whiner**

"I guess I'm a silent sufferer. For example, I never complain in a restaurant, even if the food is awful."

"Is that so? Bad food in a restaurant really annoys me. I always complain! I mean, why should I pay for terrible food? I guess I must be an activist."

B Pair work What would you do or say in these situations? Compare your answers.

1. A taxi driver is playing the radio loudly while you are trying to make a cell phone call.

2. Your neighbor's young son tore up all the flowers in your garden.

3. You see someone littering in a public park.

"If the taxi driver were playing the radio very loudly, I think I'd just speak louder. I probably wouldn't say anything to the driver. But I wouldn't give him a very good tip either."

6 I hate to mention this, . . .

role play

A Pair work Use the language in the box to create polite complaints for each situation. Then take turns acting out your complaints for the class.

1. You've been waiting in line for a long time, and someone suddenly cuts in front of you.

2. A friend always sends you jokes and chain e-mails that fill up your inbox. You like your friend a lot, but the spam is driving you up the wall.

3. After you've been waiting patiently for your food for an hour, the waiter brings you the wrong order.

4. Every time you go out with your friend, she asks you to hold her belongings because she doesn't carry a bag. It's really beginning to get on your nerves.

Useful expressions
Complaining to strangers
Excuse me, but . . .
I'm sorry, but . . .
Complaining to friends/neighbors
I hate to mention this, but . . .
I'm sorry to bring this up, but . . .

B Group work Which complaints were the most effective? Which were the most polite?

7 Letters of complaint

> Writing an effective letter of complaint is a powerful way to solve an ongoing problem with a product or service.

A Match the information to the points in the letter of complaint.

Writing an effective letter of complaint

An effective letter of complaint about a purchase . . .

1. is addressed by name to the person in charge.

2. describes the product clearly.

3. explains the problem in detail.

4. mentions a receipt or other evidence.

5. explains exactly what you want.

6. provides contact information.

May 12, 2008

Ms. Maria Lin
Customer Services Director
TZB Inc.
Center City, CA 91426 ☐ 1

Dear Ms. Lin:

Last month, I ordered a Metro MP3 player, model number 2345A, from your store's website. When it arrived, I discovered that it was broken. The connection was damaged, and the display screen was cracked.

At my own expense, I returned the MP3 player to your service department over one month ago. I still have not received my replacement, nor has a customer service representative contacted me.

I have my credit card bill to prove I paid for this purchase, a one-year warranty, and a receipt from the post office. Therefore, I would like to receive a new Metro MP3 player.

I look forward to your reply and hope you will handle this matter promptly.

Sincerely,

John Citizen
101 Bee Tree Road
Center City, CA 91426

B Write a letter of complaint using one of these situations or one of your own.

- Your digital camera came with the wrong battery charger, but you didn't notice at first. The store employee refuses to replace it.

- You bought airplane tickets in advance, but they had overbooked the flight, and you couldn't get on the plane.

C **Pair work** Take turns reading your letters. Did the writer follow all the advice for writing an effective letter of complaint?

1 Why don't they do something about it?

starting point

A How many of these problems have you experienced? Compare with a partner.

"I hate those huge SUVs that everybody's driving. What I don't get is why they can't buy a smaller car."

"Umbrellas are so poorly made these days. I don't know why they always break in the wind."

"My cell phone never works around here. I can't understand why the reception is so bad."

"The clothes in those shops are unbelievably expensive. How anyone can afford them is beyond me."

"I wonder if I'll be able to get a taxi later. It can be difficult to get one around here at night."

"The college course I want is really popular. My big concern is whether I'll be able to get into the class."

B **Pair work** Which of the problems above bother you the most? Explain.

"Broken umbrellas definitely bother me the most. That happened to me just the other day."

"You can say that again. I just hate it when that happens."

> **Useful expressions**
>
> **Agreeing and showing sympathy**
> I know (exactly) what you mean.
> Yeah, I hate that too.
> You can say that again.

2 If this is correct, say, "Yes."

listening

A Have you ever had problems with automated phone menus? What happened?

B Listen to Gabriel using an automated phone menu. Is he successful? Check (✓) the best summary.

☐ a. He completed his business successfully and will pick up his prescription this evening.

☐ b. He can't fill his prescription because the machine can't recognize what he's saying.

☐ c. His pronunciation is so poor that the system doesn't understand him.

C Listen again. Answer the questions.

1. What's the name of the store?
2. What is his prescription number?
3. What is his phone number?
4. What time does he want to pick up his prescription?

3 Simple and complex indirect questions

grammar

> Simple indirect questions use statement word order and begin with expressions such as *I wonder*, *I'd like to know*, or *I can't understand*.
>
> Will I be able to get a taxi later?   I wonder if **I'll be able to get** a taxi later.
>
> Complex indirect questions also use statement word order. In addition, they begin and end with clauses or phrases with *be*.
>
> Will I be able to get into the class?   **My big concern is** whether I'll be able to get into the class.
> How can anyone afford them?   How anyone can afford them **is beyond me**.
>
> *Grammar Plus: See page 125.*

A Look at the starting point on page 84 again. Can you find more indirect questions? Which ones are simple indirect questions? Which are complex?

B Rewrite these questions using the words in parentheses. Then compare answers with a partner.

1. Will airlines ever stop losing passengers' luggage? (I wonder . . .)

   I wonder if airlines will ever stop losing passengers' luggage.

2. How do I correct a mistake on my phone bill? (I'd like to know . . .)

3. Why can't I use my cell phone in an elevator? (The thing I don't get is . . .)

4. How can I get tickets to sold-out concerts? (I want to find out . . .)

5. When will the government deal with global warming? (I'd like to know . . .)

6. Why do people complain so much? (. . . is something I can't understand.)

4 I'm totally baffled!

vocabulary & speaking

A Look at these words that describe feelings. Put them in the columns below.

annoyed	demoralized	enraged	infuriated	mystified
baffled	depressed	frustrated	insulted	saddened
confused	discouraged	humiliated	irritated	stunned

Confused feelings	Angry feelings	Sad feelings
baffled	annoyed	

B **Pair work** Complete the sentences with your own information. Then discuss your answers with a partner.

1. I'm totally baffled by . . .   3. I always get discouraged when . . .

2. I get so irritated when . . .   4. I sometimes feel depressed when . . .

"I'm totally baffled by those online clothing sites. You never know if the clothes you order are really going to look good on you."

5 A word to the wise

discussion

A **Pair work** Read the advice about how to prevent consumer problems. Can you add any more ideas to the list?

Buyer Beware!
SMART ADVICE FOR SMART SHOPPERS

- Buy from a reputable company.
- Make sure there's a guarantee.
- Examine your purchases before you buy.
- Do some comparison shopping.
- Find out about the return policy.
- Find out how the item should be cared for.

B **Group work** Discuss a time when you had a problem with something you bought. Would the advice above have helped you?

"I bought new luggage last month, and one of the wheels has already come off."

"Oh, you're kidding. Did you take it back to the store?"

"Yes, but they told me I couldn't return it because I'd bought it on sale. I should have asked about their return policy . . ."

> **Useful expressions**
>
> **Sympathizing**
> Oh, you're kidding.
> That's ridiculous.
> What a pain.

6 I'd like to return this.

role play

A Read the store returns policy below. Is there a similar policy at the stores you visit?

B **Pair work** Now take turns role-playing a customer and a clerk at a returns counter. Use the returns policy and the information below.

> **STORE RETURNS POLICY:** All items must be in good condition and accompanied by a receipt. No cash refunds; store credit only. No items returned after two weeks unless under warranty. No return of items purchased on sale or with coupons.

Situation 1
- T-shirt
- have receipt
- shrank after washing
- now too small

Situation 2
- laptop
- receipt at home
- defective
- still under warranty

Situation 3
- camera
- lost receipt
- not very user-friendly
- want to exchange

"I'd like to return this T-shirt, please. I can't understand why it shrank after I washed it."

"I wonder whether you followed the washing instructions properly."

"I certainly did!"

"That's fine, then. May I see your receipt, please?"

Consumer watchdogs

reading

A Pair work Think of three things that could go wrong for a bride before her wedding. Read the article. Are your ideas mentioned?

Wedding Shop Leaves Brides Waiting at Altar

Every year, more than 300,000 brides in the U.K. go shopping for the perfect gown to help make their wedding a perfect day. We caught up with furious brides who would like to ask Verna and Robert Davis, the people who run the It's Your Day wedding shop in Thornbury, England, why they didn't get their dresses in time – or at all. Heather Molloy paid £650 to the Davises for a deposit on her dress. After her second visit, she realized Verna Davis was not measuring up to her expectations.

Heather said, "I had several fittings canceled or delayed for different reasons and different excuses and this went on for a period of time. I was worried because I was supposed to pick up my wedding dress two weeks before the wedding and she said, "No, no don't worry. Everything's going to be OK."

The ceremony was planned, the cake was chosen, the guests were invited, but there was still no wedding dress. Finally, on the night before her wedding, when she was supposed to be having dinner with family and friends, Heather got the call to say her dress would be ready. However, when she got there, the dress still wasn't ready. The Davises promised to work on the dress all night and deliver it first thing in the morning of the big day.

After a sleepless night, Heather had just two hours to go before her wedding and there was still no sign of the Davises. With only one hour to spare, Heather finally cut her losses – she went to the nearest wedding shop and bought a replacement dress off the rack. She never even got a refund on her deposit.

We also spoke to Robyn Brown, who is getting married two days from now. She didn't know whether or not she would receive her dress on time, so she already bought a replacement. What's more, Rachael Thorpe took the Davises to court after they supplied her with a bodice that was defective and didn't even fit her.

We have asked the Davises for a statement regarding the complaints, but so far, they haven't issued one, and we're wondering if they will.

Source: BBC Watchdog Report

B Pair work Number the events in the correct order and compare with a partner. Then take turns telling Heather's story in your own words.

____ a. Heather had to cancel a pre-wedding dinner to pick up the dress.

____ b. With only an hour to spare, Heather had to purchase a replacement gown.

____ c. At their first meeting, Heather gave the Davises a large deposit for her wedding dress.

____ d. But the dress still wasn't ready, even though the wedding was the next day.

C Group work Discuss these questions. Then share your answers with the class.

1. Do you think this report would make the Davises change their ways?

2. What could Heather have done differently?

Values

LESSON A · How honest are you?

1 What would you do?

starting point

A Look at the situations and people's responses. What would you do?

If you accidentally dented a parked car in a parking lot . . .

"If the owner weren't around, I'd leave a note with my phone number."

"I wouldn't leave a note if the owner weren't around."

If you found out your co-worker got the job using false credentials . . .

"I would keep it a secret only if I liked my co-worker."

"I would keep it a secret unless my co-worker continued lying about it."

If the ATM gave you more money than you asked for . . .

"I wouldn't tell the bank unless it were a large amount."

"Even if I were really broke, I'd return the extra money to the bank."

B **Pair work** Now read these statistics. Do you find them surprising? Why or why not?

69% of people said they would leave a note with their contact information if they dented a parked car and the owner weren't around; 31% said they wouldn't.

51% of people said they would keep it a secret if they found out a co-worker got his or her job with false credentials; 49% said they would probably tell someone.

48% of people said they would keep the extra money from an ATM; 52% said they would return it.

Source: Tickle.com Values Test; Internet survey of adults

2 Finders keepers

listening

 Listen to Aaron and Leanne talking about finding something. Are these statements true or false, or does the person not say? Check (✓) the correct answer.

	True	False	Doesn't say
1. Aaron's son wanted to keep the wallet and spend the money.	☐	☐	☐
2. Aaron's son received a thank you card as a reward.	☐	☐	☐
3. The owner of the book probably didn't care much about it.	☐	☐	☐
4. Leanne will probably return the book.	☐	☐	☐

3 Present unreal conditional with *unless*, *only if*, and *even if*

grammar

Unless clauses include exceptions that would change the speaker's decision.
I **wouldn't** tell the bank **unless** it **were** a large amount.
I **would** keep it a secret **unless** my co-worker **continued** lying about it.

Only if clauses stress the condition for the result.
I **would** keep it a secret **only if** I **liked** my co-worker.

Even if clauses are followed by unexpected results.
Even if I **were** really broke, I'd return the extra money to the bank.

Grammar Plus: See page 126.

A Look at the starting point on page 88 again. Look at the responses to the first situation. Are they different in meaning? If so, how?

B Circle the words that are true for you. Then complete the sentences.

1. If a cashier undercharged me, I (would) / wouldn't tell him if / (even if) . . .

   If a cashier undercharged me, I would tell him even if it were a small difference.

2. I *would / wouldn't* borrow a lot of money from a friend *only if / unless* . . .

3. I *would / wouldn't* return a gift I'd received to the store *if / unless* . . .

4. I *would / wouldn't* "temporarily borrow" an unlocked bicycle on the street to go a short distance *only if / even if* . . .

5. I *would / wouldn't* report my friend for skipping work *only if / unless* . . .

It's a little unethical

vocabulary & speaking

A These words describe people's ethics and attitudes. Which prefixes give them the opposite meaning? Put the words in the columns below.

acceptable	approving	fair	legal	rational	scrupulous
agreeable	ethical	honest	logical	responsible	trustworthy

dis-	il-	ir-	un-
			unacceptable

B **Pair work** Use the vocabulary words above to discuss these questions.

1. Would you ever make an international call from work to save money?

2. Would you ever play a practical joke on your friends?

3. Would you ever tell a friend with a terrible new haircut that she looks fantastic?

5 Ethical dilemmas

discussion

A Read these situations. What would you do?

What Would You Do?

1. **You've had plans for several weeks to visit your aunt. The day before, your friend invites you to a really great party the same night.**

■ Would you cancel your original plans?

■ If so, would you tell the truth or "a white lie" about why you were canceling?

■ Would you cancel your plans even if you knew your aunt were looking forward to it?

2. **You're at a convenience store, and you see someone shoplifting a can of soup.**

■ Would you tell the clerk?

■ What if the shoplifter were a woman with a small child?

■ Would it make a difference if the shoplifter looked dangerous?

3. **You're taking an evening course, so you have a student ID card. Businesses all over town give discounts to students. You work full-time during the day.**

■ Would you use the card to get the cheaper prices?

■ What if you earned a high salary at your job?

■ Would it make a difference if you were buying from a major chain store or a small mom-and-pop business?

B **Group work** Share your answers and give reasons for each. Then agree on the best course of action for each situation.

"Unless it were a special occasion for my aunt, I might leave a little earlier so I could get to the party before it ended."

6 Too good to be true

discussion

A Which of these situations seem reliable? Check (✓) those that seem honest.

☐ 1. A website offers free international phone service.

☐ 2. A company sends you an e-mail asking you to confirm your credit card details online.

☐ 3. Someone on the street asks you to sign a petition that requires your address and phone number.

☐ 4. A television ad offers a set of knives worth $300 for just $75.

B **Pair work** Discuss your experiences with these or similar situations.

"I once bought a kitchen appliance that I saw advertised on TV. The price was really good, and it worked well at first, but after a few weeks, it broke."

7 Thesis statements

writing

> A thesis statement introduces the topic of a composition. It is often located at the beginning of the first paragraph. In contrast, a topic sentence states the main idea of a single paragraph.

A Read the composition and choose the best thesis statement from the choices below. Then, write a (T) where you think the thesis statement should appear.

1. I've made some bad decisions.
2. We learn a lot from the decisions we make.
3. I have good and bad memories of old friendships.

When I'm faced with a decision that puts my ethics on the line, I think about what similar situations in the past have taught me. In my life, I've made both good and bad choices.

One of my good decisions resulted in a casual friend becoming a very close friend. A college classmate gave me a lottery ticket for my birthday. As she gave it to me, she joked that if I won, I would split the prize with her. I ended up winning $500. At the time, I was saving for a new laptop, and with the $500, I had enough money. I considered not telling her that I'd won. But I felt dishonest and disloyal, and I gave her half. I'll always be glad I did, and I wouldn't do it any differently today, even if I really needed all the money.

One of my bad decisions ruined a friendship. A former classmate wanted a job with my company and asked me to recommend her. I knew she didn't have very good work habits. I told her I would do it only if she promised to work hard. She was hired, but three months later, she was fired because my boss thought she was irresponsible and her work was unacceptable. I was fairly new at the company myself, and my company is still a little unsure about trusting my judgment now. We don't have much to do with each other these days.

I believe that good and bad decisions are a part of everyone's personal development. Is it possible to learn from those experiences? I think it is because even the bad ones help to prepare you for the future.

B Write a four-paragraph composition about a happy memory or a regret. Follow these guidelines.

1st paragraph: Begin with a thesis statement and introduce your topic in the rest of the paragraph.

2nd paragraph: Write about a decision you would make again.

3rd paragraph: Write about a decision you would make differently.

4th paragraph: End with a strong conclusion.

Your thesis statement . . .
- should contain a single idea.
- should be neither too general nor too specific.
- should unify all the paragraphs.
- can be improved as you write.

C **Group work** Take turns reading your compositions. Is the thesis statement too general? Does it need to be improved?

I wish . . .

A Read these chat room messages. Match each message with one of the values below.

a. careful spending   c. perseverance   e. rapid career advancement

b. concern for others   d. good family relations   f. good cross-cultural relations

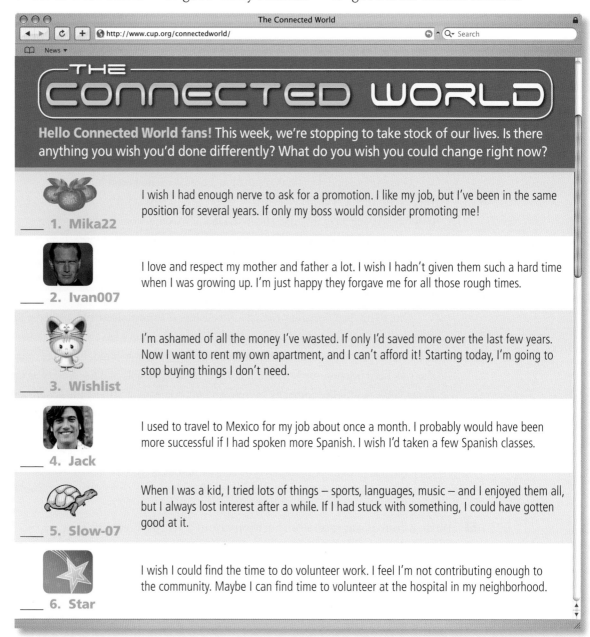

The Connected World

http://www.cup.org/connectedworld/

THE CONNECTED WORLD

Hello Connected World fans! This week, we're stopping to take stock of our lives. Is there anything you wish you'd done differently? What do you wish you could change right now?

_____ **1. Mika22**   I wish I had enough nerve to ask for a promotion. I like my job, but I've been in the same position for several years. If only my boss would consider promoting me!

_____ **2. Ivan007**   I love and respect my mother and father a lot. I wish I hadn't given them such a hard time when I was growing up. I'm just happy they forgave me for all those rough times.

_____ **3. Wishlist**   I'm ashamed of all the money I've wasted. If only I'd saved more over the last few years. Now I want to rent my own apartment, and I can't afford it! Starting today, I'm going to stop buying things I don't need.

_____ **4. Jack**   I used to travel to Mexico for my job about once a month. I probably would have been more successful if I had spoken more Spanish. I wish I'd taken a few Spanish classes.

_____ **5. Slow-07**   When I was a kid, I tried lots of things – sports, languages, music – and I enjoyed them all, but I always lost interest after a while. If I had stuck with something, I could have gotten good at it.

_____ **6. Star**   I wish I could find the time to do volunteer work. I feel I'm not contributing enough to the community. Maybe I can find time to volunteer at the hospital in my neighborhood.

B Pair work Which person in the chat room is most like you? Which of the values above are the most important? What are some of the values you learned when you were growing up?

"I'm similar to Slow-07 – I start lots of things, but I don't stick with them very long."

"My parents taught me that it was important to show concern for other people."

2 Wishes and regrets

grammar

For wishes about the present and future, use *wish* + past simple, past continuous, or *could / would* + verb.
I **wish** I **had** enough nerve to ask for a promotion.
I **wish** I **could find** the time to do volunteer work.

For regrets about the past, use *wish* + past perfect.
I **wish** I'**d taken** a few Spanish classes.
I **wish** I **hadn't given** my parents such a hard time when I was growing up.

For regrets about the past, use *if* + past perfect and *could / would have* + past participle.
If I **had stuck** with something, I **could have gotten** good at it.

For strong wishes about the present or future, or for strong regrets about the past, use *if only*.
If only clauses are often used without a main clause.
If only my boss **would consider** promoting me!

Grammar Plus: See page 127.

A Look at the starting point on page 92 again. Which sentences express regrets about the past? Which ones describe wishes for the present or future?

B Rewrite these statements using the words in parentheses. Compare answers with a partner. Are any of the sentences true for you?

1. I can't find the time to exercise. (I wish . . .)
   I wish I could find the time to exercise.

2. My grades weren't very good last semester. (If only . . .)

3. I don't know how to dance very well. (I wish . . .)

4. I didn't apply for that interesting job at work. (I wish . . .)

5. I'm feeling very stressed these days. (I wish . . .)

6. I never learned how to swim when I was a child. (If only . . .)

7. I gave away all my old CDs and DVDs last summer. (If only . . .)

8. I watched too much TV and didn't read enough when I was a kid. (If only . . .)

C Complete these sentences with your own wishes or regrets and add extra information. Then compare answers with a partner.

1. If only I had enough money to . . . ! Then I wouldn't . . .
   If only I had enough money to buy a motorcycle!
   Then I wouldn't have to take the bus to class.

2. I wish I could find the time to . . . . If I could, I would . . .

3. I wish I had learned how to . . . when I was a kid. If I had, I'd . . .

4. If only I knew how to . . . . Then I could . . .

5. I wish my friends would . . . so that . . .

6. If only I had listened to my parents when they told me . . . because . . .

7. I wish they would pass a law that says . . . . If they did, . . .

3. Personal values

vocabulary & speaking

A What words describe people's values? Complete the chart with the correct noun or adjective.

Noun	Adjective	Noun	Adjective	Noun	Adjective
compassion	compassionate		indifferent	selfishness	
	discreet	kindness		sensitivity	
generosity		resilience			tender
	honest		respectful		tolerant

B **Pair work** Which three values do you think are most important? Decide with a partner. Give your reasons.

"We thought generosity, tolerance, and honesty were most important. Generosity is an important value because if you help people, they might help you one day. Tolerance matters because . . ."

4. Three important values

listening & speaking

A 🔘 Listen to these on-the-street interviews. What values do these people think are important? Number the values in the order you hear them.

___ honesty   ___ privacy   ___ respect

B 🔘 Listen again. Whose answer did you agree with the most? Why do you think so?

"I'd say I agreed with the first woman the most. If you're not honest, you'll only get yourself into trouble. Plus, telling the truth is the right thing to do."

5. Grant me a wish.

speaking

A If you could have three wishes, what would they be? Make a list.

"My first wish would be for my family to stay healthy and happy. Second, I would wish for more peace in the world. For my last wish, . . ."

B **Pair work** Compare your wishes with a partner. Then share your answers with the class.

6. Subway Superman

A **Pair work** Read the title and the first paragraph of the news article. What would you do if you were Wesley Autrey? Discuss, then read the article.

New York HONORS A HERO

It started as a typical day for Wesley Autrey, a 50-year-old construction worker in New York City. It was about 12:45 P.M., and he was waiting on a subway platform to take his daughters home before he went to work. He suddenly noticed a man nearby have convulsions and collapse. Mr. Autrey and two women went to help the stranger. The man, Cameron Hollopeter, managed to get to his feet, but then stumbled at the edge of the platform and fell onto the subway tracks. Mr. Autrey looked up and saw the lights of the subway train approaching through the tunnel.

What would you do? Stand horrified and watch helplessly? Most people would jump in to help, but only if there were no train in sight. Mr. Autrey acted quickly. He leapt down onto the track. He realized that he didn't have time to get Mr. Hollopeter and himself back up on the platform before the train arrived, so he lay on top of the man and pressed down as hard as he could. Although the driver tried to stop the train before it reached them, he couldn't. Five cars passed over them before the train finally stopped. The cars had passed only inches from his head. His first words were to ask the onlookers to tell his daughters he was OK.

New York loves a hero. And there was no question that Mr. Autrey's actions had been just

that – heroic. He became an overnight sensation. People couldn't get enough of the story. The media named him the "Subway Superman." New York City Mayor Michael Bloomberg gave him the Bronze Medallion, the city's highest honor. (In the past, this honor has gone to such people as General Douglas MacArthur, Martin Luther King, Jr., and Muhammad Ali.) He was also asked to appear on several high-profile television talk shows.

His selfless bravery was also rewarded with money and gifts. Among other things, Mr. Autrey received: $10,000 from Donald Trump, a $5,000 gift card from the Gap clothing store, a new Jeep, tickets and backstage passes to the next Beyoncé concert, and a free one-year public transit pass. A "Disney ambassador" thanked him with a one-week all-expenses-paid trip to Disney World and tickets to see *The Lion King* on Broadway.

How did Autrey, a Navy veteran, react to all this? Honorably. He said, "I don't feel like I did anything spectacular; I just saw someone who needed help. I did what I felt was right."

B Read the article again. Are these statements true or false? Check (✓) the correct answer. Correct the false statements.

	True	False
1. Autrey hadn't noticed Hollopeter before he fell into the tracks.	☐	☐
2. There was very little space between Autrey and the bottom of the train.	☐	☐
3. Autrey jumped onto the tracks because he wanted to be a hero.	☐	☐

C **Group work** Discuss these questions.

1. Have you ever had the opportunity to help someone in trouble or in danger?
2. Why do you think so many businesses wanted to reward Mr. Autrey?

Moving around

1. The benefits of studying abroad

starting point

A Read this website. Choose three benefits of studying a language abroad that you feel are the most important.

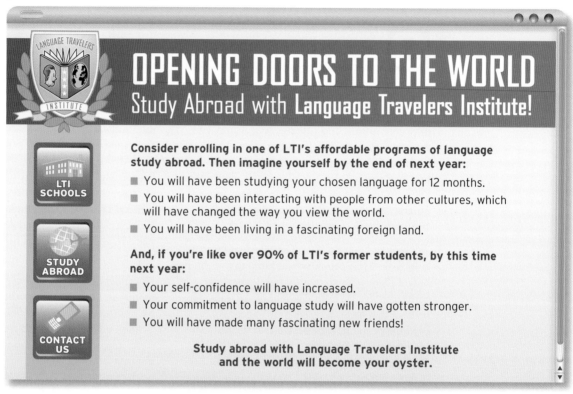

OPENING DOORS TO THE WORLD
Study Abroad with Language Travelers Institute!

Consider enrolling in one of LTI's affordable programs of language study abroad. Then imagine yourself by the end of next year:

- You will have been studying your chosen language for 12 months.
- You will have been interacting with people from other cultures, which will have changed the way you view the world.
- You will have been living in a fascinating foreign land.

And, if you're like over 90% of LTI's former students, by this time next year:

- Your self-confidence will have increased.
- Your commitment to language study will have gotten stronger.
- You will have made many fascinating new friends!

Study abroad with Language Travelers Institute and the world will become your oyster.

LTI SCHOOLS

STUDY ABROAD

CONTACT US

B **Pair work** Discuss your choices. What are some other benefits of studying or living abroad?

"I think interacting with people from other cultures is the most important benefit."

2. Words of encouragement

vocabulary & speaking

A Complete these phrasal verbs with a preposition from the box.

about	in	of	to	with

1. adjust __to__
2. be excited _____
3. be scared _____
4. be familiar _____
5. become aware _____
6. get accustomed _____
7. look forward _____
8. participate _____
9. take advantage _____

B **Pair work** What challenges do people face when they live or study abroad? Discuss with a partner using the phrasal verbs above.

"Sometimes people are scared of starting a new job abroad because they aren't familiar with the routines."

3 Future perfect and future perfect continuous

grammar

Use the future perfect to emphasize that something will be completed or achieved by a particular point in the future.
By this time next year, your self-confidence **will have increased**.

Use the future perfect continuous to emphasize the duration of an activity in progress at a particular point in the future.
By the end of next year, you **will have been studying** your chosen language for 12 months.

Grammar Plus: See page 128.

A Look at the starting point on page 96 again. Find three examples of the future perfect and the future perfect continuous tense.

B These sentences about Joon's year abroad all have mistakes. Correct the mistakes using the future with *will*, the future perfect, or the future perfect continuous. Then compare answers with a partner.

1. By this time tomorrow, Joon ~~will travel~~ *will have been traveling* for 24 hours.

2. By the end of next week, they <u>will have been installing</u> his phone. Then we can call him!

3. He'll be going out more after a few weeks because <u>he will have been more familiar</u> with the city.

4. After studying English for a few months, <u>he will have felt</u> more confident about speaking to people.

5. By this time next year, he probably <u>will not have been writing</u> us many letters, but we <u>will have continued</u> to write to him anyway.

6. I'm sure he <u>will change a lot</u> by the time he comes back to Korea.

7. His family <u>will have been</u> surprised when he gets back because he <u>will have been changing</u> so much.

8. And just think – the next time we see him, he <u>will turn</u> 22 already, and he <u>will be</u> away for a year!

C Use these time expressions to write sentences using the future perfect or future perfect continuous. Then share them with a partner.

1. Before this class ends, . . .
2. By the end of the day, . . .
3. By the end of the week, . . .
4. At the end of the semester, . . .
5. In two years' time, . . .
6. By the year 2020, . . .

4 Customs and traditions

discussion

A Read this list of Canadian customs. Are they the same or different from those where you live? Check (✓) the correct answer.

		Same	Different
1.	Both men and women shake hands with each other when they meet.	○	○
2.	Business meetings are friendly, but even so, there isn't much socializing beforehand.	○	○
3.	Lunch is usually a fairly light meal that doesn't last long.	○	○
4.	People are usually punctual for business appointments.	○	○
5.	It's common to ask people you meet what kind of work they do.	○	○
6.	Many people eat dinner early in the evening, around 6:00 P.M.	○	○
7.	People generally talk quite a bit while they're eating dinner.	○	○
8.	It's not uncommon for couples to display affection in public.	○	○
9.	Most people open gifts as soon as they receive them.	○	○
10.	When invited to someone's home, a gift, such as flowers or dessert, is always appreciated.	○	○

B Group work How do you feel about the customs above? Explain your opinions.

"I think men and women should kiss on the cheek when they meet. Just shaking hands seems kind of cold somehow."

5 When in Rome . . .

listening

A 💿 Listen to Andrew, Rachel, and Layla talking about their experiences abroad. Answer the questions.

1. What helped each of them get used to their new living situation?
2. What different things did each find difficult to adjust to?

B 💿 Listen again. Did Andrew (*A*), Rachel (*R*), or Layla (*L*) do these things? Write the correct letter.

___ 1. felt homesick

___ 2. went out for afternoon tea

___ 3. made friends at tapas restaurants

___ 4. started feeling confident about her English

___ 5. ate dinner late at night

___ 6. thought people talked about themselves too much

___ 7. enjoyed the old buildings

___ 8. watched comedy TV shows

___ 9. tried to talk about herself

6 Conclusions

writing

> The conclusion can close your composition by restating the main idea, summarizing the main points, looking to the future, making recommendations, or a combination of these methods.

A Read these two concluding paragraphs. Which methods do the writers use? Underline the parts of the conclusions that helped you decide.

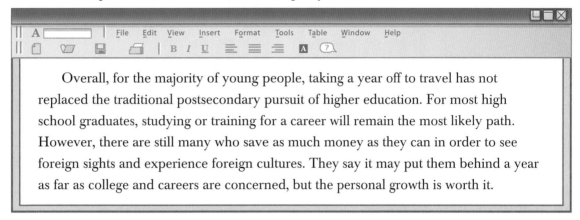

Overall, for the majority of young people, taking a year off to travel has not replaced the traditional postsecondary pursuit of higher education. For most high school graduates, studying or training for a career will remain the most likely path. However, there are still many who save as much money as they can in order to see foreign sights and experience foreign cultures. They say it may put them behind a year as far as college and careers are concerned, but the personal growth is worth it.

In brief, there are real benefits to studying abroad. While it is certainly possible to learn the language in a country where it is not widely spoken, living abroad offers limitless possibilities for improvement. Additionally, foreign students have a real opportunity to hone their life skills. Generally, they are responsible for everything from money management, accommodation, and meals to ensuring that they have a good balance between their social and school life. Studying abroad offers not only language lessons, but also life lessons, and is well worth considering.

B Find these linking words or phrases in the conclusions. How are they used? Do you know any others that have the same meaning?

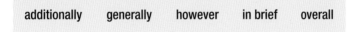

additionally	generally	however	in brief	overall

C Write a composition about living or traveling abroad. Choose one of these topics or one of your own. Your conclusion should contain at least one of the methods described above and some linking words or phrases.

- culture shock
- group travel
- independent travel
- studying abroad

D **Pair work** Exchange papers with a partner and answer these questions.

1. What methods did your partner use in his or her conclusion?
2. Are the linking words used effectively? Why or why not?
3. Can you offer any suggestions to improve your partner's conclusion?

Travel tips

starting point

A Read these people's experiences and the expert's advice. Can you think of any other advice?

TERRY'S Travel Tips

Our travel expert, Terry Tripper, responds to some troubled travelers.

A woman fell down in front of us during our sightseeing tour. While we were helping her, someone stole our money! If we hadn't been so nice, we would still have our cash!
– MARGARET, BOSTON

Terry says: I'm not nearly as nice as you! If there is a commotion, I hold on to my wallet.

And remember, sometimes the person creating the commotion is working together with the thief!

I want to share a tip my friend gave me. If you're worried about losing your passport, don't carry it around with you. Just keep it in your hotel room. – SÉRGIO, RIO DE JANEIRO

Terry says: Sorry, your friend was wrong. Keep your passport with you at all times. If someone had broken into your room, you would probably still be trying to get home!

Help! I didn't arrange anything in advance, and now I'm in London in high season, and the only hotel rooms we can find are way too expensive. – KIM, VANCOUVER

Terry says: Try a travel website. And in the future, plan before you go. If you had done some research at home, you wouldn't be having such a bad vacation now.

B **Pair work** What travel questions would you ask Terry? Tell your partner. Try to offer advice.

"I want to buy souvenirs from the places I'm going to visit, but I also like to travel light. Should I store them at the airport or somewhere else?"

"The best thing would be to mail them home. If you don't mind waiting, use surface mail or sea mail. It's cheaper."

Things went wrong.

listening

A Listen to Cindy and Scott talking about their travel problems. What happened to each person?

B Listen again. Check (✓) the statements you think are probably true. Compare your answers with a partner. Give reasons.

☐ 1. Cindy has a unique, easy-to-see name tag on her luggage.

☐ 2. Cindy travels frequently.

☐ 3. Scott likes peace and quiet when he travels.

☐ 4. Scott slept soundly all the way to Panama City.

3 Mixed conditionals

grammar

Use *had / hadn't* + past participle and *would / wouldn't* to talk about hypothetical events in the past that have effects on the present.
If we **hadn't been** so nice, we **would** still **have** our cash!
If someone **had broken into** your room, you **would** probably still **be trying** to get home!

Grammar Plus: See page 129.

A Look at the starting point on page 100 again. Find another mixed conditional sentence. Does this sentence describe actual or hypothetical events?

B Complete these sentences with the correct form of the verbs in parentheses.

1. If I ___had been___ (be) more adventurous when I was younger, I ___wouldn't have___ (not have) any regrets about the things I missed.

2. The airline lost my luggage. If I _____ (bring) a change of clothes in my carry-on bag, I _____ (not shop) for new clothes now.

3. This flight is so long! If I _____ (not buy) an economy class ticket, I _____ (be) more comfortable now.

4. If you _____ (learn) to speak some Mandarin before moving to Taipei, you _____ (be able to) ask someone for directions now.

5. If Martha _____ (not become) a flight attendant, she probably _____ (not travel) as much as she does.

4 Your own trip

discussion

A **Pair work** Have you ever had problems on vacation? Tell your partner. Consider the topics below or your own ideas.

- health
- accommodation
- food
- safety
- language
- costs
- getting around
- weather

"I went to the beach last week, but the weather was awful."

"Why? Was it rainy?"

"No, it was too sunny. If it hadn't been so sunny, I wouldn't have this terrible sunburn now."

B **Group work** Share your bad travel experiences. Get advice about what you could have done differently.

5 One word or two?

vocabulary

A Combine the items from the boxes to make compound adjectives.

culturally	assured	minded
non	aware	motivated
open	conforming	reliant
self	hearted	sensitive
	judgmental	starter

culturally aware, nonjudgmental, open-minded . . .

B **Pair work** Are the above characteristics important when you travel? Give an example for each one.

"If you're culturally aware, you'll find it easier to accept cultural differences."

6 Planning a trip

role play

A **Group work** Imagine you are planning a vacation. Discuss these questions. Write notes about what your group decides for each question.

1. Where would you like to go?
2. How long would you like your stay to last?
3. Would you like to go with a tour group or on your own?
4. What type of accommodations do you prefer?
5. What kinds of activities would you like to do during the day?
6. What sorts of evening activities would you prefer?
7. What would each person's budget be?
8. What types of transportation would you plan on using?

B **Class activity** Choose someone in your group to act as a travel agent and present your vacation to the class. The class votes on the best itinerary.

"We have planned a truly exotic vacation for you in the remote Galápagos Islands! You'll stay for seven unforgettable days in a five-star resort . . ."

Solo travel

reading

A What are the best ways to experience a new place when you travel? Make a list. Then read the article to compare your list with the author's.

Get Yourself Lost

Travelers to a new city are often encouraged to take a bus tour. The thinking is that they can later return to the places that **captivated** them, but that's nonsense! What you see from the inside of a fast-moving bus is sanitized and unreal, utterly removed from the authentic sights, sounds, and smells outside.

The best way to experience any destination is by foot, without an itinerary, wandering where your spirit leads you. Even in the largest cities, the **savvy** traveler **plunges** into the very center of town and walks down the nearest street, experiencing the actual life of the people while looking into the grocery stores and courtyards. You eventually get to many of the same sites that are on the bus route – the museums, the monuments, the city hall – but you will have witnessed so much more because you will have felt the contemporary life of the city you're visiting.

"But what if I get lost?" people ask. No one ever gets permanently lost in a major city. Eventually, a trolley or bus passes with the words "Central Station" on its front and you can easily return to the center of town. Besides, the most wonderful things can happen if you do get lost, such as stopping at a sidewalk café to sit and relax and then asking directions from the locals at the next table. Hopefully, your trip may be **enhanced** by this encounter. Here are a few ways to make the most of your travels:

▶ Know before you go. Before you depart, spend time in a library or bookstore, learning about the history and culture of your destination so you will better understand the place you're visiting.

▶ Move around like a local. Use the local subways, trams, and buses. You'll not only save money, you'll learn how people live there, and you'll gain a realistic perspective of the city.

▶ Check the bulletin boards. Bulletin boards list free lectures, concerts, workshops, and social gatherings, giving you a chance to join or meet the area's most **dynamic** residents.

▶ Take a walking tour. If you must book a guided tour, select the nonstandard, inexpensive kinds conducted on foot.

So, the next time you feel lured by a sightseeing bus tour, save your money and instead, wander around on your own. I promise you a time you'll remember fondly.

Source: "Get Yourself Lost," by Arthur Frommer

B Find the boldfaced words in the article. Then circle the correct words to complete the sentences.

1. If something **captivates** you, you're *upset / captured / delighted* by it.

2. A **savvy** traveler is *refined / experienced / adventurous.*

3. If you **plunge** into an activity, you probably *walk away from it / throw yourself into it / stumble into it.*

4. If you **enhance** your reading skills, you *upgrade / restore / prolong* them.

5. **Dynamic** people are more *cautious / unstable / interesting* than others.

C **Pair work** How do your travel habits compare with those in the article? Which ideas do you think you'll try the next time you visit a new city? Why?

How well can you do these things? Rate your ability from 1 to 5 (1 = low, 5 = high).

Talk about annoying behavior using relative clauses (Ex. 1)	_____
Make and respond to complaints (Ex. 1)	_____
Discuss what you would or wouldn't do with *unless*, *only if*, and *even if* (Ex. 2)	_____
Listen to people discussing hypothetical situations using conditionals (Ex. 3)	_____
Discuss the importance of different personality traits (Ex. 4)	_____
Talk about how life might have been different using mixed conditionals (Ex. 5)	_____

Now do the corresponding exercises below. Were your ratings correct?

Annoying customers

role play

A What do you think annoys these people about their passengers or customers?

1. bus drivers
2. flight attendants
3. tech support workers
4. waiters/waitresses

"Something that probably drives bus drivers crazy is when people complain that the buses are running late. It usually isn't their fault."

B Pair work Take turns playing the role of a customer complaining and an employee responding to the complaints.

I'd like to try . . .

discussion

A Look at these questions and write answers that are true for you.

1. What is something you'd like to try, even if it were a little risky?
2. What is something you would do only if it were a matter of life or death?
3. Where is someplace you would go if you got the chance, even if you couldn't really afford the time?

B Pair work Discuss your answers with a partner.

"I'd like to try scuba diving at night, even if it were a little risky. I think diving in the ocean at night must be incredible."

3 Training

listening

A Listen to a training workshop. What job are the trainees going to do?

B Listen again. Are these statements true or false? Check (✓) the correct answer.

	True	False
1. Sammy would try to get the customer on a flight the same day.	☐	☐
2. Andrea says the customer should have left more time between flights.	☐	☐
3. Ricardo says the customer should be ashamed she missed her flight.	☐	☐

4 Culture shock

discussion

A **Pair work** How important are these personality traits for someone who is living and working in a new culture? Number them from 1 to 6 (1 = most important, 6 = least important).

It's most / least important to be . . .

- ☐ culturally aware
- ☐ nonjudgmental
- ☐ open-minded
- ☐ self-assured
- ☐ self-aware
- ☐ self-reliant

B **Group work** Join another group and compare your results.

5 What if . . . ?

discussion

A **Pair work** Discuss the questions.

How would your life be different today if . . .

1. you'd been born in another country?
2. you'd grown up in a much smaller or larger family?
3. you hadn't learned any English?
4. you hadn't met your best friend?

B **Group work** What event or circumstance has had the biggest effect on you? How would your life be different if that event hadn't happened?

"I think growing up in an extended family had the biggest effect on me. If my grandmother hadn't been living with us, I wouldn't have such an awareness of my culture and my ancestors."

Grammar Plus

1A Verbs followed by gerunds

These verbs are followed by a gerund:
deny   discuss   finish   mention   practice   quit   resist   suggest

These verbs are followed by an infinitive:
arrange   claim   decide   demand   deserve   expect   pretend   refuse   volunteer

Some common expressions are always followed by gerunds.
She **had fun / a good time arranging** the party.
He **has trouble / a tough time getting** his assignments in on time.
He's **busy cooking** dinner right now.
She never **worries about cleaning** up after herself.

Some verbs take either a gerund or an infinitive, but the meaning of the sentence will be different.
I **stopped to drink** some coffee. (I ended one activity and began another.)
I **stopped drinking** coffee. (I don't do that activity anymore.)
I **stopped running** when I got tired. (I temporarily ended the activity.)

1 Complete these sentences with the gerund or infinitive form of the verb in parentheses.

1. I practiced _____ (speak) English with an American friend last night.

2. He volunteered _____ (help) at the hospital fund-raiser.

3. They discussed _____ (go) somewhere exotic on their vacation this year.

4. She's stopped _____ (talk) to him because they had a big argument.

5. Everyone was busy _____ (get ready) for the new school year.

6. I just can't resist _____ (give) an opinion when I disagree.

2 Circle the best answer to complete the sentences.

My friend Shanda is pretty cool and very outgoing. She's usually busy (1) *to do / doing* a million things at once. Last week, I suggested (2) *to go / going* out for dinner and (3) *to see / seeing* a movie. We arranged (4) *to meet / meeting* at 7:00. Well, I know she doesn't worry about (5) *to be / being* on time, but she didn't show up until 7:30. At first, she said it took her a long time to finish (6) *to get / getting* ready. Then, after the movie, she couldn't resist (7) *to tell / telling* me what really happened. She was having such a good time (8) *to play / playing* video games with her brother that she forgot about our plans. It's a good thing I'm the laid-back type!

Other phrases used to introduce noun clauses include *the downside of, the upside of, the hard part about, the good thing about, the only thing about, the trick to, the secret to,* and *one difficulty with.*
The downside **of** sharing a bedroom is **(that) it's hard to have any privacy.**
The hard part **about** being a twin is **(that) people are always calling you by the wrong name.**
The trick **to** living in a crowded house is **(that) you have to have a private space of your own.**
One difficulty **with** being the youngest is **(that) everyone is always telling you what to do.**

The phrases ending with a preposition can be followed by a gerund phrase, *not* **+ a gerund phrase, or a noun phrase.**
The secret to **getting along with your siblings** is (that) you have to respect their privacy.
The good thing about **not being in a big family** is (that) you always get to choose what's on TV.
The upside of **a large family** is (that) you always have someone to spend time with.
The only thing about **working moms** is (that) they have less time to spend with you.

1 Complete the sentences with *about, of, with,* or *to.*

1. The best thing ____ my grandma living with us is that she's a great cook.

2. The upside ____ being a two-income family is we can afford a few small luxuries.

3. One difficulty ____ living with my in-laws is that they want everything their way.

4. The trick ____ living in a large family is you have to learn to respect each other.

5. The hard part ____ strict parents is you always have to remember the rules.

6. The problem ____ not going to our family reunion is I won't see my cousins.

2 Rewrite the sentences. Change the noun phrases in boldface to gerund phrases.

1. The trouble with **a big family** is it's expensive to feed everyone.
   The trouble with having a big family is it's expensive to feed everyone.

2. The trick to **a two-income family** is you have to schedule family time together.

3. The hard part about **a big house** is there's so much work to do.

4. The upside of **a big house** is no one has to share a room.

5. The only bad thing about **little brothers** is I always have to baby-sit them.

6. One good thing about **little sisters** is they really look up to you.

7. One problem with **an extended family** is we had to get a bigger car.

8. The greatest thing about **a small house** is the bills are a lot lower.

2A Past modals and phrasal modals of obligation

Some past modals and phrasal modals of obligation are stronger than others.

Strong obligation. To show that there was no choice about doing the action, use *was/were to* or *had to*. Note that *must* is not used in the past. Instead, use *had to*.
My parents **had to** go to school on Saturdays.

Expectation. There was a general expectation that an action was required or prohibited.
She **was supposed to** talk to my professor after class. (But she probably didn't.)
He **wasn't supposed to** drive the car to school. (But he probably did.)

Advisability. There was a good idea or a correct action in a particular situation, but it was or was not done.
He **should have** taken better notes in class. (But he didn't.)
She **shouldn't have** bought such an expensive jacket. (But she did.)

Necessity. The action was considered to be necessary or unnecessary; however, unlike *had to*, there is a choice about doing or not doing the action.
I **needed** to make an appointment with the counselor.
I **didn't need to** buy the textbook, but I thought it looked interesting.

No obligation. There is complete choice about doing the action.
I **didn't have to** take piano lessons, but I wanted to.

1 Match the sentence on the left with the correct meaning on the right.

1. Peter shouldn't have gone to the party. ____
2. I was supposed to turn off my cell phone. ____
3. He needed a math tutor to help him study. ____
4. Ji Eun didn't have to cram for her exam. ____
5. They had to submit their work on Friday. ____
6. He wasn't supposed to stay out late. ____

a. Cramming wasn't necessary.
b. It was a bad idea to go.
c. It was necessary if he wanted to pass.
d. There was a "no cell phones" rule.
e. His parents wanted him home early.
f. The deadline was the end of the week.

2 Circle the correct answer to complete the sentence.

1. Jan *should have / shouldn't have* ignored the problem because it only got worse.

2. I *was supposed to / didn't have to* apologize, but I was too stubborn.

3. Yoko *needed to / wasn't supposed to* ignore her parents' advice, but she did.

4. He fixed the leak himself, so he *didn't need to call / should have called* a plumber.

5. When I got older, I *had to / wasn't supposed to* learn to solve my own problems.

6. Marcos *should have / shouldn't have* read the instructions before using the machine.

7. I *needed to / didn't have to* book my flight so early, but I wanted a good seat.

2B Modals with multiple uses

Degrees of certainty range from very certain to uncertain.

Very certain. To show that you think something was probable in the past, use *must have, must not have, can't have,* or *couldn't have.*
Jake had a stomachache last night after dinner. He **must have** eaten too much.
Sofia was at a movie with me last night. You **couldn't have** seen her at the mall!

Uncertain. To show that you think something was possible in the past, use *could have, may have, might have, may not have,* or *might not have.*
Jun Ho is usually here by now. He **could / may / might have** missed the bus this morning.
Tanya was supposed to meet me before school. She **may / might not have** gotten the message.

To give opinions or advice, there are a greater number of modals available for talking about the present or future than there are for the past.

Present or future. Use *must (not), have to, have got to, had better (not),* or *should (not).*
Parents **have got to** monitor the shows their children watch.
The kids **had better not** spend so much time indoors playing computer games.

Past. Use *should (not) have.*
I **should have** listened to the advice my parents gave me about having a healthy lifestyle.
We **should not have** ignored the scientists' warnings about global warming.

Circle the correct answer to complete the sentence.

1. A: Kimi didn't come to the party last night. I wonder why?

   B: I'm not sure. She *could have / should have* been sick, I guess.

2. A: Ron said he saw a UFO last night.

   B: That's ridiculous. He *couldn't have / must have* been dreaming.

3. A: I got a terrible cramp in my leg while I was jogging yesterday.

   B: Hmm. You *must not have / may have* done your stretches properly first.

4. A: I had to ask Nathalie twice to turn down the TV.

   B: She *might not have / must have* heard you the first time.

5. A: They said the meeting was at 7:30, but it had already started when I got there.

   B: They told me 7:00. You *can't have / must have* been told the wrong time.

6. A: Marnie wasn't at work yesterday. Was she sick?

   B: Well, she *couldn't have / must have* been too sick. I saw her at the park.

7. A: I'm worried about my little brother. He gained ten kilos last year.

   B: Well, he *couldn't have / shouldn't have* been eating all that junk food.

8. A: Sorry I'm late. We were playing baseball, and I didn't notice the time.

   B: You *may not have / couldn't have* been doing that. It's been dark for an hour!

3A Defining and non-defining relative clauses

That can be used for people or things in defining relative clauses. However, it cannot be used as a replacement for *where*.

Many of the people **that live in Paris** leave the city in August to vacation in other places.

A statue of ducks **that can be found in Boston** is a popular tourist attraction for children.

Pamplona is the city in Spain **where the bulls run through the streets during a summer festival**.

That cannot be used in non-defining relative clauses. *Who*, *which*, or *where* are used instead.

Cairo, **which has fascinated Europeans for ages**, draws countless European tourists each year.

Our tour guide, **who knew a great deal about souvenirs from the area**, helped us to buy some beautiful presents for our friends.

1 Complete the defining relative clauses with *that, who, when*, or *where*.

1. People _____ live in cities have more stress than people _____ live in small towns.

2. Amy likes to stay in hotels _____ there are lots of theaters and restaurants nearby.

3. Some city people have cottages by lakes _____ they can swim and relax during the summer season.

4. Many office workers like to have lunch in a park _____ they can sit in the sun and enjoy the nature _____ is all around them.

5. The city is better for students _____ want to work in the summer because it's the place _____ the job market offers the most opportunities.

6. People _____ live in towns _____ there are no movie theaters often rent movies.

2 Match the information about these cities. Then make sentences with non-defining relative clauses.

1. New Yorkers / often go to museums _c_
2. Moscow / artistic subway stations ___
3. Nagano / 1998 Winter Olympics were held ___
4. Sydney / famous for its Opera House ___
5. Venice / built on 118 small islands ___
6. Hawaii / has warm weather all year ___

a. is in the mountains of Japan.
b. is a popular winter destination.
c. seldom visit Times Square.
d. crossed by many canals.
e. the largest city in Russia.
f. also has a well-known bridge.

New Yorkers, who often go to museums, seldom visit Times Square.

3B Order of modifiers

Shape (*round, thin*), color (*red, blue*), and material (*silk, plastic*) are also used to describe nouns. They appear in the following order:

Quality	Size	Shape	Age	Color	Type	Material	Noun
quaint	little	curved					streets
picturesque			old	brightly colored	resort		hotels
	small				Japanese	wooden	fishing boats

1 Put the words in the correct order.

1. He bought a *red / house / brick / little* in the center of town.
2. They're renting a *cottage / pink / traditional / square* beside the river.
3. He hated living in a *border / town / remote / little* with its *wooden / houses / run-down*.
4. The town had many *old / buildings / cement* with *steel / dirty / black / roofs*.

3B Connecting contrasting ideas

There are three ways to connect contrasting ideas.

To begin an adverb clause, use *although* or *even though*.
I'd like to live in a small town someday **even though** I love all the opportunities in big cities.
Although I love all the opportunities in big cities, I'd like to live in a small town someday.

To begin an independent clause, use the transition words *however*, *nevertheless*, or *on the other hand*. Note the punctuation with transition words.
I love big cities. **However / On the other hand,** I'd like to live in a small town someday.
I love big cities; **nevertheless / however,** I'd like to live in a small town someday.

To begin a noun phrase, use the prepositions *despite* or *in spite of*.
Despite all the opportunities in big cities, I'd like to live in a small town someday.
I'd like to live in a small town someday **in spite of** all the opportunities in big cities.

2 Complete each sentence with a word or phrase from the box. Sometimes more than one answer is possible.

although	however	in spite of	on the other hand	nevertheless

1. This is a great city; _____ , it's too crowded.
2. _____ living downtown is expensive, there's a lot to do.
3. The summer is beautiful here. _____ , it's terrible in the winter.
4. _____ the high crime rate, I'm not afraid to walk home alone after dark.

In a reduced time clause, the subject of the clause is omitted and the verb is changed to an *-ing* form. A time clause with *before*, *after*, or *while* can be reduced only if the subject in the sentence's other clause is the same.

Before **I go to sleep**, I like to read.
Before **going to sleep**, I like to read.
I like to read before **going to sleep**.
Before **the baby goes to sleep**, **his mother reads** to him.

Once, *every time*, *till*, *as*, *the first / next / last time*, and many other phrases can all be used in time clauses. Time clauses beginning with these words and phrases cannot be reduced.

As soon as / **Once** I drink that first cup of coffee, I'm ready for the day.
Whenever / **Every time** I stay out late, I have trouble getting up the next morning.
I always stay at the office until / **till** I've finished all my work.
I like to watch TV while / **as** I'm eating dinner.
The last time I drank too much coffee, I was jittery all day.

1 Which of these time clauses can be reduced (*R*)? Which ones cannot be reduced (*N*)? Write the correct letter.

____ 1. Ever since I can remember, I've been a night owl.

____ 2. My mother races off to work right after I leave for school.

____ 3. Before he starts his day, my father has coffee and reads the paper.

____ 4. As soon as I get up in the morning, I drink a large glass of water.

____ 5. I always listen to my MP3 player while I run.

____ 6. I usually perk up for the afternoon after I eat lunch.

____ 7. Whenever I drink coffee after 3:00, I have trouble falling asleep.

____ 8. I always have breakfast at a local café before I start classes for the day.

2 Rewrite the sentences using reduced time clauses.

1. I usually read the newspaper while I have breakfast.

2. My sister won't drink orange juice after she brushes her teeth.

3. She does a lot of housework before she leaves for work in the morning.

4. Power nappers work better after they sleep for a short time during the day.

5. It's not a good idea to eat anything heavy before you exercise.

6. If I listen to soft music while I study, I can concentrate better.

7. After I've been in an argument, I need to be by myself for an hour or two.

8. Before I chill out at night, I make sure everything is ready for the morning.

The following are all additional commonly used clauses that state reasons and conditions.

Now that introduces a change in general circumstances that explains the main clause. *Now that* means *because now*.
Now that I have a job that starts early, I have to leave the house by 6:30.

Whether or not introduces a condition that might or might not occur, and which will not influence the main clause. Note its two possible positions.
She goes jogging every morning **whether or not** it's bad weather.
She goes jogging every morning **whether** it's bad weather **or not**.

Provided / Providing that introduces a condition that must be met for the main clause to be true.
Provided that I get all my schoolwork done, my weekend will be free.
Providing that I get a promotion, I'll stay with my company a few more years.

1 Match the sentence on the left with the correct meaning on the right.

1. I always have breakfast whether I'm hungry or not. ____

2. Now that she works the afternoon shift, she always has time for breakfast. ____

3. Unless her mother makes it, she doesn't bother with breakfast. ____

4. She only eats breakfast if she's hungry. ____

5 Provided that she has enough time, she has breakfast. ____

6. As long as she has breakfast, she can concentrate in class. ____

a. She has plenty of time to eat something in the morning.

b. Sometimes she skips her morning meal.

c. I eat something every morning.

d. When she is in a hurry, she doesn't eat breakfast.

e. She never makes her own morning meal.

f. If she doesn't eat, she can't think clearly.

2 Circle the correct answer to complete the sentence.

1. He won't be late for work *as long as / unless* the bus is on time.

2. *Considering that / Just in case* I took a nap, I shouldn't feel this drowsy.

3. I'll wake up on time tomorrow, *provided that / unless* I set my alarm clock.

4. He jogs after work *now that / unless* he's too tired at the end of the day.

5. My brother usually goes to bed early *now that / whether or not* he's sleepy.

6. *Now that / Even if* I'm going to bed later, I'm getting up later.

7. I'm afraid to nap at lunch *even if / just in case* I start snoring at my desk.

8. *Even if / Provided that* I'm totally exhausted, I can't sleep on airplanes.

5A Infinitive and gerund phrases

In a sentence with *It's* + adjective + infinitive, it is possible to follow the adjective with *for* and a pronoun/noun.
It's difficult for her to talk about her feelings openly.
It's customary for North Americans to make frequent eye contact.

For sentences in the negative, use *not* + infinitive or *not* + gerund.
It's considered rude **not to thank** people who give you gifts.
Not thanking people who give you gifts is considered rude.

Adjectives of feeling (*glad, happy, sad, pleased*) cannot be used with the *It's* + adjective + infinitive structure. Instead, the sentence needs to say who has (or doesn't have) these feelings.
Most parents are both happy and sad to see their children grow up.
People are always delighted to get compliments.

1 Rewrite the sentences using infinitive or gerund phrases.

1. It's important to make a good first impression.

   Making a good first impression is important.

2. Arriving late for an appointment is inappropriate in most countries.

3. It's fairly typical for college students to get to a party late.

4. It's considered rude not to be punctual for a dinner party.

5. Keeping the conversation going is easy for Elyse.

6. Showing the bottom of your feet is offensive in some places.

7. It's good form to bring a small gift to a dinner party.

8. Talking about politics is sometimes risky.

9. It's customary for parents to brag about their children.

10. Calling to thank the hostess the day after a party is a nice idea.

2 Write sentences with infinitive phrases using the words below.

1. Tom / always happy / loan money to his friends.

   Tom is always happy to loan money to his friends.

2. Wendy / unusual / arrive late to class.

   It's unusual for Wendy to arrive late to class.

3. encouraging / struggling students / receive good grades in school.

4. Min / always glad / help a friend in need.

5. many tourists / surprised / learn about some American customs.

6. students / inappropriate / interrupt a teacher.

7. new employees / often afraid / ask their bosses for help.

8. dinner guests / customary / thank their hosts.

9. businesspeople / important / be punctual for appointments.

10. Eun Mi / never shocked / see people eating on the subway.

The modals *can*, *may*, *must*, *have to*, and *don't have to* change in reported speech. *Might* and *should* do not change. Also notice how the pronouns change in reported speech.

Statements	Reported statements
"You **can** go to the party with **me**."	She said I **could** go to the party with **her**.
"I **may** go to a movie tonight."	He said he **might** go to a movie tonight.
"We **must** tell him the truth."	They said they **had to** tell him the truth.
"He **has to** go to the bank."	He said he **had to** go to the bank.
"You **don't have to** pay me back.	She said I **didn't have to** pay **her** back.
"We **might** get married."	She said they **might** get married.
"I **should** replace **my** old laptop.	He said he **should** replace **his** old laptop.

Say and *tell* are used differently in reported speech. *Tell* must be followed by a noun or object pronoun. *Say* is not followed by a noun/pronoun object.

Statements	Reported statements
"Don't park the car there."	She **told me** not to park the car there.
	She **said** not to park the car there.

When a very recent statement is being reported, no tense change is necessary.
A: I didn't hear that. What did she say?
B: She said she **wants** to go out for dinner.

Change these conversations to reported speech.

1. **Ryan:** I'm thinking of applying for a promotion at work.
   Emma: What kind of promotion is it?
   Ryan: Our department needs a new manager.
   Emma: You should definitely apply!
   Ryan: I'm a little nervous because there's a big interview.
   Emma: You just have to practice. I can help you.

   Ryan told Emma he was thinking of . . .

2. **Karl:** Do we have to sign up for our after-school club today?
   Mrs. Chu: You can sign up until noon tomorrow.
   Ava: Don't wait too long. The good ones are filling up fast.
   Karl: I'll do it after I eat my lunch.

6A Present perfect vs. simple past

Use the present perfect to report a repeated past event.	Use the present perfect to report an event that has an effect on the present, or is still relevant.
Thieves **have robbed** three banks this year.	She**'s been** more careful since she lost her car keys.
The seal **has painted** four pictures so far.	The shop **has had** a security camera for six months now.

1 Complete these sentences with the simple present or the present perfect form of the verbs in parentheses.

1. The police _____ (catch) him when he _____ (sell) the stolen art.

2. Unbelievably, the same woman _____ (win) the lottery twice.

3. So far, the children _____ (raise) more than $500 for charity.

4. Since the city _____ (pass) its new laws, crime _____ (fall).

5. The kidnappers _____ (not call) and _____ (demand) any ransom yet.

6. No storms _____ (strike) since summer _____ (begin).

6A Present perfect vs. present perfect continuous

Some verbs, such as *live, work, study, give / take (lesson)*, and *teach,* express the idea of an ongoing action. They can usually be used in either the present perfect or the present perfect continuous.
He **has lived** in London for eight years.
He **has been living** in London for eight years.
I have taken violin lessons since I was three.
I have been taking violin lessons since I was three.

2 Review the rules for the present perfect and the present perfect continuous on page 45. Then circle the correct form of the verb to complete the article. Sometimes more than one answer is possible.

It's a sad day for many who (1) *have lived / have been living* in the town of Meaford since they were children. The town (2) *has decided / has been deciding* to take down the old fishing pier. Fisherman Bob Kates said, "I (3) *have worked / have been working* here since I was young. Generations of kids (4) *have taken / have been taking* swimming lessons here. I myself (5) *have jumped / have been jumping* off this pier many times, especially on hot summer days. Take today for example. The temperature (6) *has already reached / has already been reaching* 36 degrees, but already the town (7) *has put up / has been putting up* barriers. It's true that the pier (8) *has been / has been being* in pretty bad condition for a while now, so I guess it's a safety issue."

It's not all bad news for Mr. Kates. The town (9) *has studied / has been studying* proposals for replacing the pier for a year now, and in fact, planning for a new and improved pier (10) *has already begun / has been beginning*.

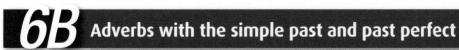

When and the simple past and past perfect can be used to express different time relationships.
When I arrived in Bangkok, my connecting flight **had already departed**.
When I arrived in Bangkok, my friend **met** me at the airport.

When *before* makes the sequence of events clear, simple past or past perfect can be used.
It began to rain before she **boarded** the plane.
It began to rain before she **had boarded** the plane.

Yet and *already* are used with both present and past perfect to show that an event took place before now.
It **had already started** raining when I arrived in Bangkok.
It **hadn't started** raining **yet** when I arrived in Bangkok.

Circle the correct answer to complete the story.

The taxi arrived to take Erica to the airport for her flight to London. (1) *Until that day / After that* she (2) *was never / had never been* on an international flight. The travel agent (3) *told / had told* her to get to the airport early, so she (4) *arrived / had arrived* four hours before her flight was due to leave. When she (5) *got / had gotten* there, she (6) *realized / had realized* she had plenty of time to spare, so she (7) *decided / had decided* to have some coffee and a snack and look at the newspaper before she (8) *checked / had checked* in. She (9) *already / had already* bought some chocolate bars to eat on the plane, so she decided to have one of those. She sat at the counter and ordered a coffee.

When her coffee (10) *came / had come*, she pulled her favorite section out of the newspaper, carefully refolded it, and put it on the counter beside her. When she (11) *reached / had reached* for her chocolate bar, she saw that someone (12) *already took / had already taken* it out of the package and (13) *broke / had broken* it into eight tidy squares. She looked beside her and saw a distinguished-looking businessman. Before that, (14) she *didn't really notice / hadn't really noticed* him. She watched as he picked up a piece of the chocolate and calmly popped it into his mouth. Up until then, she (15) *never saw / had never seen* such rude behavior, so still staring at him, she (16) *picked up / had picked up* a piece and ate it. By now, he was staring back. He picked up another piece and ate it. So did Erica. Finally, there was only one piece left. Erica (17) *took / had taken* it.

The man stood up. He said, "Look. If you're that hungry, buy yourself a donut!" He (18) *slammed / had slammed* a dollar bill down on the counter and stormed out. In her entire life, she (19) *was never / had never been* so shocked before. Muttering to herself, Erica began to gather up her things. Suddenly, she stopped, standing as still as a statue. There, under her newspaper, (20) *was / had been* her chocolate bar, exactly where she (21) *put / had put* it before the whole fiasco began.

If the agent (the person or thing doing the action) is unknown or obvious from the context, it's better to use a passive form. However, if the person or thing doing the action needs to be emphasized, it's better to use an active form.

The virus **was sent** to disrupt Internet service at the college. (unknown agent)
College degrees **are being offered** online. (agent is clear from context)
Bill Gates **started** Microsoft, not Bill Clinton! (emphasize the agent)

The passive cannot be used with the present perfect continuous. Use the passive of the present perfect instead.

People **have been downloading** more music this year than ever before.
More music **has been downloaded** this year than ever before.
Even more music **will have been downloaded** by this time next year.

1 For each pair of sentences, is it better to use the passive or active form?
Circle *a* or *b*.

1. a. More U.S. employers will probably block access to Internet video sites.
   b. Access to Internet video sites will probably be blocked.

2. a. Soon, inventors will invent devices to download movies in under a minute.
   b. Devices to download movies in under a minute will be invented soon.

3. a. Automakers might be including Internet access in their products soon.
   b. Internet access might be included soon.

4. a. Bloggers are creating blogs on a wide range of topics.
   b. Blogs are being created on a wide range of topics.

2 Complete the sentences with the correct active or passive form of the verb in parentheses.

1. Recently, chat rooms _____ (become) popular with all age groups.

2. Every week, freeware _____ (download) on computers everywhere.

3. Soon, podcasts _____ (watch) by more and more night-shift workers.

4. Lately, people in remote areas _____ (ask for) more hot spots.

5. More sophisticated computer viruses _____ (create) all the time.

6. For years, hackers _____ (try) to use spyware to commit identity theft.

7. In the future, more college classes _____ (broadcast) over the Web.

8. Recently, blogs _____ (use) to spread gossip about movie stars.

7B Negative and tag questions for giving opinions

Use past negative and tag questions to get an opinion about a past event.
Didn't you think the manager's speech was a little boring?
The manager's speech was a little boring, **didn't you think?**
The manager's speech was a little boring, **wasn't it?**
The manager has given some pretty boring speeches, **hasn't he?**
The manager's speech had just put everyone to sleep when the fire alarm rang, **hadn't it?**

In informal spoken English, *they* **can be used as the pronoun in tag questions when the subject is** *somebody, someone, everybody, everyone, nobody,* **or** *no one*.
Almost **everyone** has a cell phone these days, don't **they?**   Yes, they do.
Somebody has hacked into your computer, haven't **they?**   Yes, they have. / No, they haven't.

Use an affirmative tag question when the subject is a negative, such as *nobody* **or** *nothing*.
Nobody left any voice mail messages, **did they?**   Yes, they did. / No, they didn't.

1 Turn the statements into negative questions.

1. It would be great if telemarketers didn't call at dinnertime.

   It would be great if telemarketers didn't call at dinnertime, wouldn't it?

2. It's awful how so much paper is wasted on fliers that nobody reads.

3. That infomercial we watched was ridiculous.

4. Office towers should have to turn out all their lights at night.

5. There used to be pay phones on almost every corner downtown.

6. He had been thinking of getting a new computer.

7. Kids should spend less time playing video games.

8. Some people get really addicted to computer games.

2 Complete the sentences with tag questions.

1. Internet hoaxes are pretty commonplace lately, _aren't they_ ?

2. There haven't been any laws about using a cell phone in the car, _____ ?

3. There's something wrong with your computer, _____ ?

4. You shouldn't give your computer password to anyone, _____ ?

5. There's nothing you can do with an obsolete computer, _____ ?

6. No one ever actually clicks on those banner ads, _____ ?

7. She had already complained about the telemarketers, _____ ?

8. A personal robot that does your chores would be awesome, _____ ?

8A Reduced relative clauses

Non-defining relative clauses with *be* can be reduced in the same way as defining relative clauses. Notice the use of commas.

Albert Einstein, **who is thought to be one of the greatest minds of the twentieth century,** struggled in school.
Albert Einstein, **thought to be one of the greatest minds of the twentieth century,** struggled in school.

David E. Kelley, **who is well known for his television courtroom dramas,** used to be a lawyer.
David E. Kelley, **well known for his television courtroom dramas,** used to be a lawyer.

1 Complete the sentences on the left with the phrases on the right. Choose two phrases for each sentence.

1. A person who works as a fashion designer should be __b__ and __d__.

2. A person who is working as an accountant has to be ____ and ____.

3. A person who works as a forest ranger needs to be ____ and ____.

4. A person who is working as a taxi driver must be ____ and ____.

a. a good driver
b. aware of trends
c. knowledgeable about plants and animals
d. familiar with different styles
e. good with numbers
f. familiar with city streets
g. physically fit
h. very accurate

2 Now rewrite the sentences with reduced relative clauses.

A person working as a fashion designer should be aware of trends and familiar with different styles.

3 Rewrite these sentences using reduced relative clauses.

1. The photographer who lives upstairs has won many awards for his creativity.

2. Professional cooking, which is a tough business, requires both patience and skill.

3. Movie stars who are constantly hounded by the press deserve more privacy.

4. Tiger Woods, who is probably the world's best golfer, is very disciplined.

5. The Summer Olympics, which are held every four years, are broadcast around the world.

6. Models who are considered too thin by health experts set a bad example for girls.

8B Non-defining relative clauses as sentence modifiers

Non-defining relative clauses can be used as sentence modifiers and can contain almost any verb. Some of the most common ones are *surprise*, *depress*, *encourage*, *suggest (that)*, *contribute to*, and *result in*. Note that the verbs which describe emotion must be followed by an object.

My husband refused to get an MP3 player, **which has resulted in a closet full of old CDs.**
My teacher praised my English today, **which encourages me to study harder.**
My dad is happier since he took up golf, **which suggests that hobbies are good both mentally and physically.**
I learned how to clean jewelry with toothpaste, **which depressed me because it meant I had wasted a fortune on expensive cleaners.**
I've started making my own clothes, **which has contributed to financial savings and a full closet!**

1 Match these statements with the appropriate non-defining clauses.

1. I use dental floss to string beads for jewelry, ____

2. My sister always loved school, ____

3. Al moved to a small town, ____

4. I just had a big fight with Ana, ____

5. Paolo is really good at solving problems, ____

6. Amy jogs every morning, ____

7. I've had a private tutor for the past few months, ____

8. I want to take my own computer to class, ____

a. which surprised us since he loves cities.

b. which has contributed to weight loss and more energy.

c. which is why I have so much of it.

d. which is why people always go to him for help.

e. which has resulted in better grades for me.

f. which encouraged her to go into teaching.

g. which means I'll have to start saving for a laptop.

h. which depressed me because she's my best friend.

2 Complete the sentences with a phrase from the box.

which resulted in	which suggested	which depressed
which encouraged	which means	which surprised

1. I'm working late tonight, _which means_ I'll take a later train home.

2. My friend was in a local play, _____ me to try acting.

3. Our team lost the championship, _____ me and my friends.

4. Prices went down last year, _____ savings for many people.

5. Ted sent me a nice birthday card, _____ me since he usually doesn't do anything special for people's birthdays.

6. I burned the dinner, _____ that I had made a mistake.

9A Clauses and phrases showing contrast and exception

The following are additional common phrases that show contrast and exception.

Use *whereas*, especially in formal writing, to present contrasting information.
Whereas the bottled water market is huge in Italy, it is very small in Japan.

Use *except (for)* or *with the exception of* to show an exception within a group.
Everyone in the school, **except for** the basketball team, must attend classes this afternoon.
Everyone in the school, **with the exception of** the basketball team, must attend classes this afternoon.

1 Circle the correct answer to complete the sentence.

1. *While / Unlike* Leo prefers a big breakfast, I just have coffee.

2. No one in the class, *except that / with the exception of* Eva, can speak German.

3. *In contrast to / While* city people, people who live on farms must have a car.

4. *Unlike / Except for* Thai women, Spanish women greet each other with a kiss.

5. I'm a typical Canadian, *whereas / except for the fact that* I don't like hockey.

6. I have to be home by 9:00, *whereas / unlike* my brother can stay out late.

7. Everyone on our street, *except that / except for* my family, has a dog.

8. *Unlike / While* me, all my friends are addicted to reality shows on TV.

2 Read about Alonzo and Jun. Complete the sentences. Sometimes more than one answer is possible.

Alonzo . . .	Jun . . .
is in his last year of high school.	is in his first year of college.
considers himself to be pretty typical.	doesn't think he's really typical.
is really into all kinds of sports.	doesn't play any sports.
isn't crazy about baseball.	doesn't watch any sport but baseball.
hates using a computer.	spends a lot of time playing computer games.
avoids using his cell phone.	never goes anywhere without his cell phone.

1. Jun has already finished high school, _____ Alonzo still attends one.

2. Alonzo considers himself to be pretty typical, _____ Jun doesn't.

3. _____ Jun, Alonzo is a big sports fan.

4. Alonzo is a fan of most sports _____ baseball.

5. Jun enjoys computers, _____ Alonzo hates using them.

6. _____ Alonzo, Jun carries a cell phone at all times.

7. Alonzo probably has a lot of energy, _____ Jun doesn't seem to.

8. Jun and Alonzo are very different, _____ they both have cell phones.

9B Past habitual with *used to* and *would*

To ask questions about a repeated action or situation in the past, use *Did you use to*.
Did you use to listen to rock music when you were younger?
Did you use to share a bedroom with your little brother?

Use the negative question *Didn't you use to . . . ?* to confirm a guess about repeated actions or situation in the past.
Didn't you use to work at a grocery store after school?
Didn't he use to play on the school soccer team?

1 Write the questions for these statements.

1. A: _Did you use to live in San Francisco?_

   B: Yes, I did. I lived in San Francisco for about two years.

2. A: _____

   B: A lot? No, as a matter of fact, I've never drunk coffee.

3. A: _____

   B: No, he never did. Actually, Pete's allergic to dogs.

4. A: _____

   B: In the school band? Yes, I did. I played the flute.

5. A: _____

   B: Yes, I always rode my bike in elementary school, but I'd take the bus on rainy days.

6. A: _____

   B: Yeah, it was really long, but I had to cut it when I joined the swim team.

2 Use the words to write questions using *use to*.

1. Lesley / visit Brazil / regularly
   Didn't Lesley use to visit Brazil regularly?

2. we / have fun / during the summer holidays

3. you / want / live / in a foreign country

4. Serena / hang out / the mall every weekend

5. your parents / own / restaurant

6. you / volunteer / hospital

7. Alex / spend a lot of time / principal's office

In some relative clauses, the relative pronoun (*who, that,* or *which*) can be omitted.

In an **object relative clause**, a relative pronoun (*who, that,* or *which*) is optional. Relative pronouns are only required when they function as the subject of a relative clause.
I told a friend a secret. He told the secret to all our classmates.
I told a friend a secret (**that**) he told to all our classmates.

In a **subject relative clause**, a relative pronoun (*who, that,* or *which*) is necessary because it functions as the subject of the relative clause.
I have a roommate. She never cleans the kitchen.
I have a roommate **who** never cleans the kitchen.

1 Check (✓) the sentences where the relative pronoun (*who, that,* or *which*) is optional.

___ 1. One thing that makes me sick is really selfish people.

___ 2. People who chew gum loudly really get on my nerves.

___ 3. The restaurant that we had dinner at last night overcharged us.

___ 4. Someone's cell phone kept ringing all through the movie that I saw last night.

___ 5. I had a big argument with a store clerk who refused to give me a refund.

___ 6. My teacher gets mad at every little noise that our class makes.

___ 7. The town fined a neighbor who burned garbage in her backyard.

___ 8. The people in the line which he tried to cut into complained to the theater manager.

2 Complete the sentences with *who* or *that*. If the pronoun can be omitted, write ✗. Sometimes more than one answer is possible.

1. One thing ___ gets me down is people ___ lie to me.

2. I like people ___ stand up for something ___ they believe in.

3. Something ___ makes me sad is people ___ have no place to live.

4. Something ___ I can't do is keep up with technology.

5. I was a kid ___ had parents ___ made a lot of rules.

6. The thing ___ aggravates me most is people ___ are cruel to animals.

> If the beginning clause of an indirect question is in statement word order,
> the sentence is a statement and ends with a period.
> **I'm curious about** why he didn't complain to the landlord.
> **I'm not sure** who is responsible for repairing the roads.
> **The big question is** how we can get the city officials to listen to our concerns.
>
> If the beginning clause of an indirect question is in question word order,
> the sentence is a question and ends with a question mark.
> **Do you have any idea** how long it takes to get a passport?
> **Could you tell me** where I can go to pay my parking ticket?
> **Don't you wonder** how a place with such poor service stays in business?

1 Rewrite these sentences using the words in parentheses.

1. Why can't the city add more street lights? (I don't understand . . .)
2. Is the city going to improve the rush hour bus service? (Do you know . . .)
3. Why are prices going up so fast? (. . . is something that baffles me.)
4. How can I finish the work before the deadline? (I have no idea . . .)
5. Have you saved enough money for school? (Would you mind telling me . . .)
6. Why aren't there any bike paths in the city? (. . . is beyond me.)
7. How am I going to pay the rent this month? (My main problem is . . .)
8. When are they going to build a new hospital? (Do you have any idea . . .)
9. Who decided to close the swimming pool in the park? (Don't you wonder . . .)
10. Is tuition going up again next year? (I have to find out . . .)

2 Rewrite these sentences as direct questions.

1. I haven't got a clue what we're supposed to do for homework tonight.
   What are we supposed to do for homework tonight?
2. How people can mistreat animals is mystifying to me.
3. What I don't get is how I can keep up with all this new technology.
4. Why the government doesn't outlaw spam is my number one question.
5. I'd like to know who should be responsible for keeping our city clean.
6. Tell me what I have to do to get my driver's license.
7. When the next meeting will be is something I haven't found out yet.
8. I wonder if I should complain about my neighbor's loud parties.

11A Present unreal conditional with *unless, only if,* and *even if*

To ask a follow-up question after a yes / no question, a shortened conditional can be used, especially in spoken or informal English. The positive shortened conditional is *if so,* and the negative shortened conditional is *if not.*

Would you consider lying to a good friend to avoid hurting your friend's feelings? **If so,** what kinds of things would you lie about?

Are you sure your friends are loyal and trusting? **If not,** you shouldn't tell them your personal secrets.

1 Match the yes / no questions on the left with the follow-up questions on the right.

1. Would you say anything if a colleague called you by the wrong name? ____

2. If the man next to you on the bus fell asleep on your shoulder, would you wake him? ____

3. Would you remain silent if you disagreed with your boss in a meeting? ____

4. Would you report it if you saw a friend shoplift a small item from a store? ____

5. If someone you secretly disliked invited you to a party at her home, would you go? ____

6. If a cat always came to your house for food, would you keep it? ____

a. If not, what would you say?

b. If not, would you confront your friend?

c. If so, what would you say?

d. If not, would you try to find its owner?

e. If so, how would you wake him?

f. If not, what excuse would you give?

2 Circle the correct answer to complete the sentence.

1. I wouldn't lie to a friend *unless / only if* it was in his best interests.

2. If you found money on the street, would you turn it in to the police? *If so / If not,* what would you do with it?

3. Would you report a small theft *only if / even if* the person looked poor? *If so / If not,* would you tell the store manager, or would you call the police?

4. He wouldn't lose his temper *only if / even if* he were really angry.

5. Would you confront a friend who gossiped about you behind your back? *If so / If not,* what would you say?

6. I wouldn't read anyone else's mail *even if / only if* I were really curious.

7. Would you make a promise if you already knew you couldn't keep it? *If so / If not,* what would you do later when you didn't keep the promise?

8. I would criticize my friends *unless / only if* I knew a way to help them improve.

11B Wishes and regrets

Wishes and regrets often use comparative words, such as *(not) enough*, *more*, *less*, and *better*, and intensifiers, such as *really* and *very*.

I did**n't** save **enough** money last summer.
I wish I had saved **more** money last summer.

I spent **too much** money on video games last year.
If only I had spent **less** money on video games last year.

I bought **too many** clothes on the weekend.
I wish I had bought **fewer** clothes on the weekend.

I do**n't** understand math very **well**.
I wish I understood math **better**.

I got **really** angry at my friend last night.
If only I had**n't** gotten **so** angry at my friend last night.

1 Complete the wishes and regrets with a word from the box.

better	fewer	harder	less	more	so

1. I don't have enough time to do volunteer work.

   I wish I had _____ time to do volunteer work.

2. I don't know how to swim very well.

   I wish I knew how to swim _____.

3. I drank too much coffee before bed last night.

   If only I had drunk _____ coffee before bed last night.

4. Tom didn't study very hard for his exam.

   Tom wishes he had studied _____ for his exam.

5. Our class has too many assignments this week.

   I wish our class had _____ assignments this week.

6. I felt really sleepy in class and couldn't pay any attention.

   I wish I hadn't felt _____ sleepy in class and had paid attention.

2 Rewrite these sentences using the words in parentheses.

1. I wasn't very obedient in elementary school. (I wish . . .)
2. I refused to take piano lessons when I was young. (If only . . .)
3. I fell asleep at the computer last night, and now my essay is late. (I wish . . . Then . . .)
4. I exercised too much yesterday, so now I feel really tired. (If only . . . Then . . .)
5. Bob is shy and doesn't make friends very easily. (Bob wishes . . .)
6. I'm not a very good cook. (If only . . .)

12A Future perfect and future perfect continuous

When using the future perfect or future perfect continuous, the particular point in the future is often referred to in another part of the sentence.

By this time next year, your commitment to language study is going to have gotten stronger.
On August 1st, I will have been living overseas for six months.
After a few months, you're going to have been making real progress with English.
Before next spring, he will have finished most of his course work.
Marisa's flight will have left **soon**.
When the van arrives, I will have been packing for two days, and I probably won't have finished.
Before I leave for Paris, I will already have sold my house and put my things in storage.
After I finish this, I will have completed everything on my "to do" list.

1 Underline the words that refer to a point in the future.

1. <u>By the spring</u>, Nate will have visited over a dozen different countries.

2. When the end of the week arrives, I will have written four exams.

3. Pretty soon I'll have been working on this puzzle for an hour. It's impossible!

4. I can't believe he's still sleeping! At 11:00, he'll have been sleeping for 12 hours.

5. When she leaves for the club, she'll have changed her outfit six times.

6. If it continues, on Tuesday it will have been raining for three weeks.

7. After I finish this, I will have painted three of the rooms in my house.

8. Even before the plane lands, we will have been in the air for seven hours.

2 Complete the sentences with the future perfect or the future perfect continuous form of the verb in parentheses.

1. By the end of class, I _____ (learn) about the future perfect tense.

2. By the year 2020, I _____ (work) in my career for several years.

3. Before she's 30, Sue _____ (make) her first million dollars.

4. At the end of his trip, Seth _____ (visit) four different countries.

5. After I finish this book, I _____ (read) it for over a month.

6. By 11:00, how long _____ Dan _____ (watch) TV?

7. When I finish college, I _____ (be) in school for 16 years.

8. Pretty soon, I _____ (wait) for her for an hour. I'm getting annoyed!

9. We're late. By the time we get there, they _____ (finish) dinner.

10. On Friday of this week, Kara _____ (travel) for two months.

12B Mixed conditionals

Conditionals can appear in many forms. They can describe how situations in the past affect situations in the past, the present, or the future.

Use a past tense in both the *if* clause and the result clause to talk about true events in the past.
When I was younger, if I **didn't behave** well, my parents **were** disappointed.
If we **got** lost during our trip last year, we just **asked** someone for directions.

Use *had / hadn't* and *would / wouldn't* + present perfect to talk about hypothetical situations in the past that had effects on the more recent past.
If I **had been born** with a good voice, I **would have started** my own band a long time ago.

Use *had / hadn't* + past participle and *would / wouldn't* + verb to describe hypothetical situations in the past that have effects on the present.
If I **had studied** harder when I was in school, I **would have** a better job today.

Use *had / hadn't* + past participle and *would / wouldn't* + verb to talk about hypothetical situations in the past that have effects on the future.
If she **had booked** her flight before now, she **would be** in Paris next week.
If I **hadn't taken** a year off from school, I **would be graduating** this June.

Complete these sentences with the correct form of the verbs in parentheses.

1. As a kid, I always _____ (enjoy) school if I _____ (like) the teacher.

2. If I _____ (study) harder last year, I _____ (not have to) repeat the course this year.

3. If he _____ (not speak) Greek, his trip to Athens last year _____ (be) so enjoyable.

4. When I was young, if I _____ (see) a scary movie, I _____ (have) bad dreams.

5. When I was a kid, if my father _____ (go away) on a business trip, he always _____ (call) at 8:00 to say good night to us.

6. If I _____ (spend) less money when I was younger, I _____ (have) a nice little nest egg in a few years.

7. If I _____ (not have) a fight with my friend yesterday, I _____ (go) to the party tonight.

8. If she _____ (show) more interest since she was hired, she _____ (get) the next promotion.

9. If I _____ (not lose) my passport, I _____ (fly) to Lisbon tonight.

10. If she _____ (not start) figure skating when she was four, she _____ (not be) in the 2006 Olympics.

Units 1-12 Self-study

Unit 1 Self-study

1. Type A and Type B personalities

listening

A **Track 1** Listen to a psychology lecture about "Type A" and "Type B" personalities. What is the main difference between Type A and Type B personalities? Check (✓) the correct answer.

☐ a. Type A personalities are more successful than Type B personalities.

☐ b. Type A personalities are more concerned about goals and deadlines.

☐ c. Type A personalities are more likely to have heart attacks.

B Listen again. Are Type A people (*A*) or Type B people (*B*) more likely to do these things? Write the correct letter.

____ 1. worry about being late   ____ 3. accept small mistakes

____ 2. be content with their lives   ____ 4. feel guilty about failing

C Look at this excerpt from the lecture. Why does the professor say this? Check (✓) the correct answer. Then listen again and check.

Student: So, basically, you're saying that all the rich and famous are Type A. Politicians, movie stars, executives, all those successful people. Right?

Professor: Well, I wouldn't exactly put it like that. What I mean is . . .

☐ a. She wants to correct the student's grammar.

☐ b. She doesn't want to say whether she agrees or disagrees with the student.

☐ c. She wants to correct the student without embarrassing him.

2. Describing emotions and behavior

vocabulary

CD-ROM Look at the audio script of the lecture on page 142. Use your CD-ROM dictionary to find the words in boldface from the lecture that have these definitions.

1. to cause anger or extreme annoyance in (someone)   *exasperate*

2. able to change or be changed easily according to the situation   _____

3. lacking confidence and doubtful about their own abilities   _____

4. pleased with your situation and not needing or desiring it to be better   _____

5. using strong, forceful methods especially to sell or persuade   _____

6. showing strong dislike; unfriendly   _____

Unit 2 Self-study

1. The Nasca Lines

listening

A 🔊 **Track 2** Listen to a conversation between two students. What are the Nasca Lines? Check (✓) the correct answer.

☐ a. They're alien spaceship decorations.

☐ b. They're very old drawings on the ground.

☐ c. They're something in Clare's geography test.

B 🔊 Listen again. Check (✓) the theories you hear mentioned about why the Nasca Lines were built.

☐ a. to teach archeology   ☐ d. to teach methods of construction

☐ b. to be alien landing strips   ☐ e. to be used in religious ceremonies

☐ c. to be a guide to the stars   ☐ f. to be paths between religious sites

C 🔊 Look at this excerpt from the conversation. What is George's opinion of this theory? Check (✓) the correct answer. Then listen again and check.

George: The article I read said they must have been built by aliens so they could land their spaceships!

☐ a. He thinks it's an interesting idea.

☐ b. He thinks it's a crazy idea.

☐ c. He thinks it's a good explanation.

2. Understanding meaning from context

vocabulary

A CD-ROM Look at the words in boldface in the audio script of the conversation on page 142. Use the context of the sentences to decide if each word is a noun (*N*) or an adjective (*A*). Write the correct letter. Use your CD-ROM dictionary.

1. doubtful ____   3. geometric ____   5. stakes ____

2. enclosures ____   4. pelican ____   6. theory ____

B CD-ROM Now use the context of the sentences to guess the meanings of the words. Match the words to the definitions. Use your CD-ROM dictionary to check.

a. doubtful	b. enclosures	c. geometric	d. pelican	e. stakes	f. theory

1. a large, fish-eating bird with a throat that is like a bag   *d*

2. thick, strong, pointed wood or metal poles pushed into the ground   ____

3. uncertain or unlikely   ____

4. something suggested as a reasonable explanation for something   ____

5. consisting of shapes such as squares, triangles, or rectangles   ____

6. areas surrounded by a fence or other structure   ____

Unit 3 Self-study

1. London

listening

A 🔘 **Track 3** Listen to a training session. Who is the session for?
Check (✓) the correct answer.

☐ a. tourists   ☐ b. environmentalists   ☐ c. travel agents

B 🔘 Listen again. Are these statements true or false?
Check (✓) the correct answer.

	True	False
1. The population of London is 27 million.	☐	☐
2. The London area contains 30 percent green space.	☐	☐
3. There are fewer than 5,000 restaurants in London.	☐	☐
4. The most popular free tourist attraction is Tate Modern.	☐	☐
5. The London Eye is a Ferris wheel.	☐	☐
6. It rains more in Paris than it does in Tokyo.	☐	☐

C 🔘 Look at this excerpt from the training session. Why does the trainer say this? Check (✓) the correct answer. Then listen again and check.

Participant 1: When I was in London, it rained all the time!

Trainer: **I know what you mean, but, actually,** compared to other capital cities, London has a relatively low rainfall . . .

☐ a. He wants to politely disagree with the person.

☐ b. He wants to explain that he has been to London too.

☐ c. He wants to embarrass the person in the audience.

2. Guidewords

vocabulary

CD-ROM A guideword tells you one of the basic meanings of a word. They appear in parentheses in your CD-ROM dictionary. For each of these sentences, choose the correct guideword for *draw*.

1. But what really draws our clients to London? _c_	a. picture
2. The criticism drew an angry response from the mayor. ____	b. move
3. We can draw some conclusions about the causes of this disease. ____	c. pull/pull in
4 He drew his gun and waved it around. ____	d. take out
5. As we drew near, a dog started to bark. ____	e. decide on
6. The child drew a picture of a dog. ____	f. cause

Unit 4 Self-study

1. Dreams

listening

A **Track 4** Listen to a lecture on sleep and dreams. What is the main focus of the lecture? Check (✓) the correct answer.

☐ a. why we dream ☐ b. the stages of sleep ☐ c. reviewing for a test

B Listen again. Match the stages of sleep on the left with the notes on the right.

Stage 1 ____	a. Deep sleep. Delta waves only.
Stage 2 ____	b. Deep sleep. Mixture of Delta waves and smaller, quicker waves.
Stage 3 ____	c. Eye movements stop; brain waves slow.
Stage 4 ____	d. Fast eye movement and breathing; muscles paralyzed.
Stage 5 ____	e. Light sleep. People in this stage are easy to wake up.

C Look at this excerpt from the lecture. How does the professor feel about Phil falling asleep during her lecture? Check (✓) the correct answer. Then listen again and check.

Professor: Actually, could someone nudge Phil? He seems to be nodding off.

☐ a. annoyed ☐ b. amused ☐ c. angry

2. Word building

vocabulary

A **CD-ROM** In the listening, the professor mentions "historical research." *Historical* is a form of the word *history*. Which form of *history* completes each of these sentences? Use your CD-ROM dictionary to help.

1. The new film version of *Hamlet* features ____ accurate costumes.　　a. historian
2. The library has an important collection of ____ documents.　　b. historic
3. We visited several ____ buildings and monuments.　　c. historical
4. This biography of Gandhi was written by a well-known ____ .　　d. historically

B **CD-ROM** Use your CD-ROM dictionary to mark the word stress on each of the words in these word families. Underline the correct part of the word.

1. <u>his</u>tory　　historian　　historic　　historical　　historically
2. photo　　photograph　　photographer　　photographic　　photography
3. demonstrate　　demonstration　　demonstrative　　demonstrator

Unit 5 Self-study

1. Intercultural communication

listening

A 🔘 **Track 5** Listen to a lecture about intercultural communication. How would you summarize the lecturer's introduction? Check (✓) the correct answer.

☐ a. Different cultures have different communication rules.

☐ b. Not all cultures have communication rules.

☐ c. Cultural rules are the same; some people just don't pay attention to them.

B 🔘 Listen again. Complete this student's notes.

> Intercultural communication. How what we say affects other people. Different rules. Nonverbal communication features:
>
> 1. speaking _____   3. _____
> 2. speaking _____

C 🔘 Look at this excerpt from the lecture. Why do the students laugh when the professor says this? Check (✓) the correct answer. Then listen again and check.

Professor: And we all know how that works in our own culture – well, *most* of us know how that works in our own culture . . .

☐ a. The professor made a mistake.

☐ b. One of the students made a mistake.

☐ c. The professor was making a joke.

2. American and British English

vocabulary

CD-ROM Use your CD-ROM dictionary to match the British English words on the left with the American English words on the right. Tip: Look up the British English words.

British English	American English
1. crisp ___	a. Band-Aid
2. CV ___	b. elevator
3. holiday ___	c. faucet
4. lift ___	d. garbage
5. pavement ___	e. potato chip
6. plaster ___	f. résumé
7. rubbish ___	g. sidewalk
8. tap ___	h. vacation

Unit 6 Self-study

1. Vacation story

listening

A 🔘 **Track 6** Listen to two friends talking about a recent vacation. Where did the woman spend most of her vacation? Check (✓) the correct answer.

☐ a. Athens ☐ b. Pireaus ☐ c. an island

B 🔘 Listen again. Are these statements true or false? Check (✓) the correct answer.

	True	False
1. Libby enjoyed her vacation.	☐	☐
2. Piraeus is a Greek island.	☐	☐
3. The bus driver had a good sense of humor.	☐	☐
4. The soccer team laughed all the way to the airport.	☐	☐
5. Libby missed her flight.	☐	☐

C 🔘 Look at this excerpt from the conversation. How does John feel about the story? Check (✓) the correct answer. Then listen again and check.

John: Oh, really? Why was that?

☐ a. He's interested in it. ☐ b. He's not very interested in it.

2. Strong adjectives

vocabulary

CD-ROM In the conversation, Libby uses the phrase "pretty amazing" to mean very surprising. Use your CD-ROM dictionary to match the adjectives on the left with the stronger adjectives on the right. (Tip: Look up the stronger adjectives.)

1. boring _i_   a. astounding
2. busy ___   b. critical
3. funny ___   c. elated
4. happy ___   d. engrossed
5. important ___   e. fascinating
6. interested ___   f. hectic
7. interesting ___   g. hideous
8. ugly ___   h. hilarious
9. unexpected ___   i. tedious

Unit 7 Self-study

1. Hi-tech travel

listening

A **Track 7** Listen to the news report and answer the questions. Check (✓) the correct answer.

1. What did Scott and Matt try to do?
   - ☐ a. visit 50 countries in 50 days
   - ☐ b. visit 50 capital cities in 50 days

2. Did they succeed?
   - ☐ a. Yes, they did.
   - ☐ b. No, they didn't.

B Listen again. Circle the word or phrase you hear in each sentence.

1. News of their trip spread quickly *by word of mouth / from north to south* . . .

2. . . . and were flown down the Pacific coast of Alaska on a charter flight that tourists would pay *hundreds, if not thousands, of / a hundred thousand* dollars for.

3. People went miles *out of the way / out of their way* to help them . . .

4. After *116 / 160* rides . . .

5. . . . having traveled nearly *24,000 / 204,000* miles . . .

C Look at this excerpt from the story. Why does the announcer say this? Check (✓) the correct answer. Then listen again and check.

Announcer: Isn't the kindness of strangers incredible?

- ☐ a. He is asking for confirmation of a fact he's fairly sure about.
- ☐ b. He is asking for information about a topic he doesn't know well.
- ☐ c. He is expressing his opinion about a subject.

2. Negative prefixes

vocabulary

A CD-ROM In the listening, words like *unlikely* and *incredible* take negative prefixes. Which negative prefixes do you think each of these words takes? Use your CD-ROM dictionary. (Tip: Search for *literate, *loyal, *like, etc.)

1. ___literate   4. ___grateful   7. ___patient
2. ___loyal   5. ___comfort   8. ___regular
3. ___like   6. ___probable   9. ___similar

B CD-ROM Which of the words above have these meanings? Write the correct word. Use your CD-ROM dictionary.

1. Not showing or expressing thanks, especially to another person _____

2. Not willing to wait for something _____

3. Not knowing how to read or write _____

4. Having parts of different shapes or sizes _____

5. To find something unpleasant _____

Unit 8 Self-study

1 Creative problem solving

listening

A 🔘 **Track 8** Listen to a conversation between Hannah and Luke. What is the main topic of their conversation? Check (✓) the correct answer.

☐ a. cooking and cleaning problems

☐ b. musical inventions

☐ c. clever ideas and inventions

B 🔘 Listen again. Check (✓) the inventions or discoveries the people discuss.

☐ a. polishing shoes with banana peels   ☐ d. a device for peeling artichokes

☐ b. a dry cleaning machine   ☐ e. the electric guitar

☐ c. cleaning a hat with cornmeal   ☐ f. the frying pan

C 🔘 Look at this excerpt from the conversation. Why does Luke say this? Check (✓) the correct answer. Then listen again and check.

Luke: "Throw a few handfuls of cornmeal on the hat and dry-clean in the usual way, rubbing it in with a cloth." The usual way?

☐ a. He thinks it's funny.

☐ b. He thinks it's confusing and irritating.

☐ c. He's worried that it might damage the hat.

2 Bright ideas

vocabulary

A CD-ROM Match these phrasal verbs from the listening with their definitions. Use your CD-ROM dictionary.

1. (be) into ___   a. to invent something new by using a lot of imagination
2. come up with ___   b. to obtain knowledge of something
3. dream up ___   c. to stop doing or to stop having something
4. find out ___   d. to suggest or think of an idea or plan
5. give up ___   e. strongly interested in or involved with something

B CD-ROM Check (✓) the parts of speech that these words from the listening can be. Use your CD-ROM dictionary.

	Noun	Verb	Adjective	Adverb
1. pretty			✓	✓
2. peel				
3. stuck				
4. table				
5. throw				

Unit 9 Self-study

1 Historic figures

listening

A 💿 **Track 9** Listen to a conversation between two friends. What is Makayla doing?

☐ a. writing a note to an elementary school

☐ b. writing notes for a talk

☐ c. writing a paper about Nelson Mandela

B 💿 Listen again. Complete Makayla's notes.

> Nelson Mandela was born in a little (1) _____ in Cape province, South Africa, in (2) _____ .
>
> Studied and became a (3) _____ , but best known for being a political (4) _____ . Spent more than (5) _____ years in prison, fighting apartheid. [Apartheid = (6) _____ in Afrikaans.]
>
> Released from prison in (7) _____ . Awarded Nobel Peace Prize in (8) _____ . Elected President of South Africa in (9) _____ ; retired in (10) _____ .

C 💿 Look at this excerpt from the conversation. Why does Carla say this? Check (✓) the correct answer. Then listen again and check.

Carla: Wasn't he born in Johannesburg?

☐ a. She doesn't think Makayla is right.

☐ b. She's giving an opinion.

☐ c. She's asking for information.

2 Suffixes

vocabulary

A **CD-ROM** In the conversation, Makayla says, "*Apartheid* means 'apartness.'" The suffix -*ness* changes an adjective into a noun. Do these suffixes form nouns (N) or adjectives (A)? Write the correct letter. (Tip: Search for *able, *er, *or, etc.)

1. -able __A__   3. -hood ___   5. -ity ___   7. -ment ___

2. -er, -or ___   4. -ist ___   6. -ive ___   8. -ous ___

B **CD-ROM** Complete the sentences with the words in parentheses and one of the suffixes above. Use your CD-ROM dictionary to check your answers.

1. Nelson Mandela was a ___prisoner___ for more than 25 years. (prison)

2. He was also a political _____ . (active)

3. He is an exceptionally _____ person. (fame)

4. He became an icon of fairness and _____ . (equal)

5. He spent his _____ in Cape province. (child)

Unit 10 Self-study

1 Complaining

listening

A 🔘 **Track 10** Listen to a radio program about making complaints. What is the purpose of the program? Check (✓) the correct answer.

☐ a. to help people locate the right person to complain to

☐ b. to help people complain more

☐ c. to help people make their complaints more effective

B 🔘 Listen again. Complete the golden rules for complaining.

1. Be _____ in your own _____ about _____ you are dissatisfied.

2. Be _____ in your own mind _____ you want to _____ as a _____ of this complaint.

3. _____ _____ _____ you should complain to.

C 🔘 Look at this excerpt from the program. What does the announcer mean? Check (✓) the correct answer. Then listen again and check.

Announcer: You won't be eating *there* again, will you?

☐ a. She is fairly certain Chris will eat there again.

☐ b. She is fairly certain Chris won't eat there again.

☐ c. She isn't sure whether Chris will eat there again.

2 Feeling angry

vocabulary

CD-ROM The caller, Chris, says, "I go in there and right away I'm annoyed." Put these words with similar meanings to *annoyed* in the correct column. Use your CD-ROM dictionary to help.

bothered	enraged	irritated
disgruntled	furious	livid

Somewhat angry	Very angry

Unit 11 Self-study

1. Positive psychology

listening

A **Track 11** Listen to two students talking about a university course. Are these statements true or false? Check (✓) the correct answer.

	True	False
1. Positive psychology is a new name for conventional psychology.	☐	☐
2. Anna is interested in the course.	☐	☐
3. Maria is studying psychology.	☐	☐

B Listen again. Check (✓) the values or emotions you hear mentioned.

☐ a. generosity   ☐ e. kindness

☐ b. courage   ☐ f. optimism

☐ c. gratitude   ☐ g. patience

☐ d. honesty   ☐ h. politeness

C Look at this excerpt from the conversation. What does Maria mean? Check (✓) the correct answer. Then listen again and check.

Maria: But I'm not sure you really need a course.

☐ a. Maria thinks Anna is taking too many courses already.

☐ b. Anna has enough credits and doesn't need any more courses.

☐ c. Maria thinks Anna is a very positive person.

2. Values and character traits

vocabulary

CD-ROM Look at the words in boldface in the audio script of the conversation on page 147. Use your CD-ROM dictionary to find the words that have these definitions.

1. an uncomfortable feeling of worry _____

2. physical or mental pain _____

3. caring only about what you want or need _____

4. the ability to control fear _____

5. the tendency to be hopeful _____

6. a strong feeling of appreciation _____

Unit 12 Self-study

1. Culture shock

listening

A **Track 12** Listen to a talk about culture shock for people who are going to volunteer overseas. According to the speaker, what are the three stages of culture shock?

1. The _____ stage. You're fascinated by new and different experiences.
2. The _____ stage. You have to cope with stress and problems.
3. The _____ stage. You get used to your new environment.

B Listen again. Are these statements true or false? Check (✓) the correct answer.

	True	False
1. The culture shock talk was the second session in the program.	☐	☐
2. There were two types of sessions in the program.	☐	☐
3. The volunteers are going to be earning good salaries.	☐	☐
4. The speaker thinks that the volunteers will cope with culture shock.	☐	☐

C Look at this excerpt from the talk. What does the speaker mean? Check (✓) the correct answer. Then listen again and check.

Trainer: They're a bit rude, actually. Cold. Not like people back home. Now here come the stereotypes.

☐ a. Cultural differences can cause people to misunderstand each other.

☐ b. Foreigners aren't popular where the volunteers are going.

☐ c. Stereotypes are correct interpretations of cultural differences.

2. Verbs and prepositions

vocabulary

A Look at the verbs in boldface in the audio script of the lecture on page 147. Which preposition follows each verb?

about	to	from	in	with	for

1. benefit ____   4. succeed ____
2. cope ____   5. joke ____
3. prepare ____   6. adjust ____

B **CD-ROM** Use your CD-ROM dictionary to find out which prepositions go with each of these verbs. Sometimes more than one answer is correct.

1. apply ____   4. depend ____
2. approve ____   5. disagree ____
3. believe ____   6. worry ____

Self-study audio scripts

Unit 1 Self-study

Professor: OK, good morning, everyone. The main concept I want to cover today is the difference between two personality types, "Type A" and "Type B" personalities. Now, let me just quickly summarize this.

Type A personalities are always in a hurry, always concerned about meeting deadlines and goals. So they can get pretty impatient. They expect a lot out of other people, too. It's very easy to **exasperate** them if you make even a tiny mistake. They can be **aggressive**, even **hostile**. But they also work very hard, and a lot of them are high achievers. So – oh, Luke, do you have a question?

Student 1: So, basically, you're saying that all the rich and famous are Type A. Politicians, movie stars, executives, all those successful people. Right?

Professor: Well, I wouldn't exactly put it like that. What I mean is that Type A people can be very insecure. And because they're **insecure**, success is very important to them. They feel guilty if they don't succeed. But not all of them actually succeed. And also, not all successful people are Type A personalities.

OK, so that's the Type A personality. The Type B personality, on the other hand – well, this person is basically everything the Type A person isn't. Type B people are patient and relaxed. They're not as concerned about goals and deadlines and success. They're more likely to be **content** with the life they have. And they're more **flexible**. Other people's mistakes don't bother them as much. Any questions so far?

Student 2: Yeah, uh, when were these terms developed? And by who?

Professor: Well, it's a funny thing. The terms "Type A" and "Type B" were first used about 50 years ago by medical researchers. They were actually studying heart disease. They thought Type A personalities would have a greater risk of having a heart attack. But, in fact, later research has shown that this isn't exactly true. And a lot of psychologists don't like using the terms "Type A" and "Type B." But "Type A" and "Type B" have become common phrases we hear all the time, anyway.

Now, if you open your books to page . . .

Unit 2 Self-study

George: Hi, Clare. I'm just going to make a cup of coffee. Do you want one? What are you doing?

Clare: I should be studying for my geography test. I mean, I was. But then I picked this up and now I can't put it down.

George: What is it?

Clare: It's a book about the Nasca Lines in Peru. It's absolutely amazing.

George: I read something about them once. They're really long, straight lines that can only be seen from the air, right?

Clare: Yeah, well, some of them are the lines – the longest one is nine miles long – and others are **geometric** shapes like circles and triangles. Those are called geoglyphs. Then there's another type of drawing, called biomorphs. They're huge drawings of plants and animals. There's a spider, a monkey, a **pelican**... The pelican is 1,000 feet long!

George: The article I read said they must have been built by aliens so they could land their spaceships!

Clare: I know. But the ground is way too soft to land anything on. Someone also thought that they could have been a guide to the stars. But that's **doubtful**, too. The best **theory**, I think, is that the biomorphs were built as special **enclosures** for religious ceremonies. The lines were paths between the sites.

George: How old are they, anyway?

Clare: Nobody knows for a fact, but some archeologists think the animals and plants were constructed around 2,000 years ago, and the lines and geometric shapes about 500 years after that.

George: How could they have done that without modern machines? I mean, how do you draw a perfectly straight line nine miles long?

Clare: Well, they could have figured that out. It's not that difficult, even with simple tools. They probably used wooden stakes. They could have put two **stakes** in a straight line, then put a third one along that line. Then they must have just repeated that over and over again. Taking one stake out and putting it in front of the other, for miles. They might have drawn the biomorphs much smaller to start with, then divided them up into sections. Then they could have redrawn each section to scale . . .

George: Stop. My brain hurts. Forget the coffee. You don't need any. But I do.

Unit 3 Self-study

Trainer: Good afternoon, everyone. I hope you had an interesting and productive morning. And a good lunch! And that we can cover a lot of ground as we travel across London in our city seminar this afternoon. The more we know about the cities in our travel packages, the happier our clients will be!

London, which has twenty-seven million overnight visitors every year, is the world's most popular city destination. We used to think of London as a city of fish-and-chips-eating tea drinkers hurrying through a foggy, crowded city that has seen better days. Maybe some of us still do. But, seriously, now that many of us here today have visited this vibrant, cosmopolitan city, we know better. Can anyone tell me what the population of London is? Yes, you in the third row.

Participant 1: I think it's seven or eight million, right?

Trainer: That's right. And what about green space – any idea how much of the city is parkland? No? Green space makes up a whopping 30 percent of the London area. London has over 6,000 restaurants. And is it all fish and chips? Absolutely not. There are restaurants serving food from over 50 different countries.

But what really draws our clients to London? Primarily historical sights and museums, yes. But they're visiting new attractions, too. Tate Modern, which has free entry to one of the most important collections of modern art in the world, has become the most popular tourist attraction in London. It has about 5 million visitors a year. Has anyone here been to the London Eye?

Participant 2: What is it?

Participant 3: It's a huge Ferris wheel on the River Thames. Fantastic views.

Trainer: That's exactly right. It is huge – 135 meters tall. And the views are stunning. It's become the most popular paid-for attraction in London since it opened at the turn of the century. And speaking of the River Thames – taking a boat tour is still one of the finest ways to experience the city . . . weather permitting, of course.

Participant 1: When I was in London, it rained all the time!

Trainer: I know what you mean, but, actually, compared to other capital cities, London has a relatively low rainfall – about half as much rain as Tokyo and a third as much as Paris!

OK, now we've got a great virtual tour of London . . .

Unit 4 Self-study

Professor: OK, so before I get started, there are just a couple of announcements. Remember that there will be an exam on Monday. Then the next lecture after that will be on why we dream, so print out the notes for that lecture next.

Student 1: What's going to be covered in the exam?

Professor: Basically, everything that we've covered since October, including today's topic. After I've finished the lecture, we can have a quick question and answer session. Please hold your questions until then.

Right. So I'd like to start by going through the stages of sleep, then go on to discuss a little historical research into when we dream and finish up with current thinking about that.

So, while we are asleep, we normally pass through five stages. The first stage is light sleep. It is easy to wake people during Stage 1 sleep. Actually, could someone nudge Phil? He seems to be nodding off. Phil there was in Stage 1 sleep. Did you see how he jumped? That's due to a sudden muscle contraction, and right before that Phil probably experienced a sensation of starting to fall. Right, Phil? Yes? It's very common, we've all probably felt that. Thanks for the demonstration.

In Stage 2 sleep, our eye movements stop. And brain waves, the brain's electrical signals, slow down. In Stage 3 sleep, there is a mixture of very slow, long Delta waves and small, fast waves. Then in Stage 4, Delta waves take over completely. Stages 3 and 4 are deep sleep states. It's difficult to wake someone while they're in Stages 3 or 4. This is also the point when sleepwalking may occur.

Right, so next is Stage 5, or REM, sleep. What does R-E-M stand for – anyone?

Student 2: Rapid Eye Movement?

Professor: That's right. And, as the name suggests, the eyes are moving quickly. Breathing gets faster and our muscles are temporarily paralyzed. Most dreaming takes place during REM sleep. Until quite recently, it was thought that dreaming only occurred during REM sleep, but that has been shown not to be the case.

OK. So can anyone tell me how many times a night the average person dreams?

Student 2: We dream about six times a night, don't we?

Professor: That's right. Most teenagers and adults, basically anyone over ten years of age, dreams at least . . .

Unit 5 Self-study

Professor: OK, we're going to move on to intercultural communication. Now, intercultural communication – what is that about? Well, we'll look at how what we say affects what people think of us and what we think of other people. Now, every culture has its own rules for communication. And we all know how that works in our own culture – well, *most* of us know how that works in our own culture, even though we might not be consciously aware of it.

However, although every culture has rules, the rules aren't the same in every culture. This gives rise to all kinds of misunderstandings. For example, someone may be considered polite in his or her own culture or extremely rude in another, just because of the way he or she says something.

So, let's talk about intercultural communication. First we're going to look at a few features of nonverbal communication: speaking distance, speaking volume, and interruptions.

A nice example of speaking distance and speaking volume is to compare American and British English speakers. People in the U.S. tend to stand farther away from the person they're speaking to than British people. And they speak more loudly as a result. So the British speaker thinks that the American is loud and aggressive. People in the U.S. may feel crowded by British speakers standing too close to them.

The next feature I'd like to discuss is interruptions or turn-taking. This can be another big area of misunderstanding. We're going to try a little role play now . . .

Unit 6 Self-study

John: So, how was your trip to Greece, Libby? You look terrific.

Libby: Great. Really good, we had a lot of fun.

John: Where were you?

Libby: Well, we flew to Athens, and then after a few days there, we caught a ferry to this great island. We were on the island for about a week, I think.

John: Is it easy to travel around?

Libby: Yeah, very easy. Although we did have a pretty amazing bus trip from Piraeus, the port city where the ferry comes in, to the airport, on the way back.

John: Oh, really? Why was that?

Libby: Well, we got off the ferry at about ten o'clock, then we walked to the bus stop. There's a big sign that says "Express bus to the airport every 20 minutes." But we waited for about an hour. While we were waiting, a whole soccer team from one of the other islands showed up.

John: Really?

Libby: Yeah. They had huge bags and there were about 20 of them, all in matching track suits, looking very serious and official. At first, anyway.

John: Yeah?

Libby: Yeah, so then the bus arrives and everybody gets on. It was really crowded. Then the bus driver tells us to pass our tickets up to be punched. Well, nobody could move, so we just had to pass them hand over hand, one by one, up to the front of the bus where he punched them, very slowly. That took another ten minutes.

John: Amazing.

Libby: We were getting a little worried about missing the check-in for the flight but then we eventually got moving. So, there must have been some problem with the buses that night because all the way to the airport, people were standing in the street waiting for buses, you know, trying to flag the bus down. And the bus driver pulls over at every stop, opens the doors and shouts, "I can't stop here! This is an *express bus*!" Then shuts the doors right in people's faces and speeds away!

John: So he stopped to tell them he couldn't stop?

Libby: Exactly. It happened about eight times. And he was so serious! By about the third time he did it, the passengers around us started giggling. Then, the next time he did it, we all started laughing. Some of the soccer players were actually crying with laughter by the time we got to the airport . . .

Unit 7 Self-study

Announcer: And now the story of two Canadians who hitchhiked to all 50 capital cities in the U.S. in 50 days with more than a little help from newfound friends, cell phones, and the Internet.

After finishing college, Scott MacDonald and Matt Fiddler decided to set out with a camera and tripod, cell phone with GPS system, and no real plan, apart from a determination to meet a lot of new people, visit all 50 capitals, and not to pay for transportation.

In fact, when asked by one interviewer how they planned to hitchhike to Hawaii, they said that they didn't have a plan and "would cross that bridge when they came to it," to which the interviewer replied, "But that's the problem – there's no bridge!"

They set up a website so that people could track them. They began their trip in Times Square, New York City, where they were offered their first ride from a man named Dave. Dave had been watching them on the website and thought it was unlikely that they'd be able to get a ride out of Times Square if he didn't pick them up.

News of their trip spread quickly by word of mouth and over the Internet. They had numerous radio interviews and met many of their future rides while on the air.

They were given a private tour of the Pentagon, were invited into people's homes, were taken to dinner and to parties, and were flown down the Pacific coast of Alaska on a charter flight that tourists would pay hundreds, if not thousands, of dollars for.

They rode in cars, trains, buses, on motorcycles, airplanes, and boats. People went miles out of their way to help them get to all 50 state capitals, sometimes taking the day off work.

People were unbelievably generous. "This is one of the things that amazes us most, how people will go out of their way to help a stranger accomplish a goal," they said.

After 116 rides, they did get to Hawaii, having traveled nearly 24,000 miles at an average of 20 miles an hour. Isn't the kindness of strangers incredible?

Unit 8 Self-study

Luke: Hey, Hannah, look at this old farmhouse cookbook I found in the attic. It must have been grandma's.

Hannah: I didn't know you **were into** cooking, Luke.

Luke: I'm not. But this book has a lot of household tips which are really ingenious. Very clever.

Hannah: Such as?

Luke: "Brown shoes always look well-polished if rubbed each morning with the inside of a banana peel. Leave them to dry and then polish with a dry cloth."

Hannah: You don't have any brown shoes.

Luke: I know that. That's not the point. It's just clever, that's all. How about this one: "To clean a white hat, place the hat on a clean table or paper. Throw a few handfuls of cornmeal on the hat and dry-clean in the usual way, rubbing it in with a cloth." The usual way?

Hannah: Yeah, it makes you wonder how someone suddenly decided to try polishing their shoes with a banana peel or throwing corn meal on their hat.

Luke: How about the resourceful person who **found out** that if you peel about a hundred leaves off an artichoke, there's eventually something worth eating. Why didn't they **give up**?

Hannah: They were just hungry, I guess. What about the electric guitar? How do you **come up with** a bright idea like that? "Oh, I'll just stick some electric wires on this and see what happens . . ."

Luke: Apparently, that's pretty much what happened. I was reading about it the other day. This musician who played Hawaiian music **dreamed it up**. He made it on his dining room table. He called it "the frying pan."

Hannah: Neat. What would you like to invent?

Luke: I don't know. Maybe a transporter so you could be beamed from one place to another – no need for air travel, no pollution. I'll tell you something I wish I *had* invented – Velcro.

Hannah: Yeah. Wasn't the inventor inspired by burrs or something that stuck to his clothes while he was walking his dog?

Luke: I guess somebody that smart deserves to be a multi-millionaire. Maybe we should get a dog . . .

Unit 9 Self-study

Carla: Hi, Makayla, what are you working on?

Makayla: Oh, hi, Carla. I'm making some notes for this talk for my teaching practice session at the elementary school tomorrow.

Carla: What are you going to talk about?

Makayla: Well, the kids are doing a unit on heroes, you know, people who really challenged the status quo or stood up for something they believed in. I thought I'd talk about Nelson Mandela, then ask them to talk about people they admire.

Carla: Sounds good. Mandela really did confront big issues – and he certainly challenged the status quo. What are you planning to say?

Makayla: Well, I thought I'd start with the basic facts. You know, where he was born, when, what he studied, and so on.

Carla: Wasn't he born in Johannesburg?

Makayla: No, he was born in a little village in Cape province in 1918. He went to a mission school and then on to a boarding school. Did you know he was a lawyer?

Carla: No, I didn't. I knew he was a political activist and rebelled against apartheid. And that he went to prison, of course.

Makayla: That's right. He spent over 25 years in prison. He said, "The struggle is my life." *Apartheid* means "apartness" in Afrikaans, apparently. Hmm. I think I need to explain that to the kids.

Carla: So when did he get out of prison?

Makayla: He was released in 1990 by de Klerk, the President of South Africa at the time.

Carla: Weren't they given the Nobel Peace Prize together?

Makayla: Yes, they were. They were jointly awarded the prize in 1993, I think. Yes, 1993, then Mandela was elected President in 1994.

Carla: How long was he President? About four years?

Makayla: Five. He retired in '99.

Carla: What an exceptional life.

Makayla: Absolutely. It says here that *Time* magazine's list of the 100 most influential people in the world describes him as "one of just four people who have shaped the history of both the 20th and the 21st centuries."

Carla: Who are the others?

Makayla: Bill Gates, Oprah Winfrey and . . .

Unit 10 Self-study

Host: Hello and welcome to The Complaints Coach, where we help you complain effectively and efficiently. Now, before we take any calls, let's just run through the golden rules of complaining. There are only three, so they aren't tough to remember.

Number one: Be clear in your own mind about why you are dissatisfied. Are you unhappy about the way you were treated? Are you annoyed about someone's behavior? Were they rude or careless? Were you sold defective goods? What went wrong exactly?

Rule number two: Be clear in your own mind what you want to happen as a result of this complaint. Do you want an apology, a different decision, a refund, or a replacement? Get this straight before you complain – it's important – and make sure you tell the person you are complaining to what result you want.

Finally, rule number three: Find out who you should complain to. You should, of course, try to resolve the problem directly with the company involved. For instance, by returning the faulty product to the store where you bought it. You should either take your complaint to the relevant senior manager or to customer service. This usually works. However, if it doesn't, you may want to consider taking it further by contacting the authorities. Or, you might want to give us a call, as Chris has done this evening. Hello, Chris.

Chris: Hi. Well, I'd like to complain about this restaurant – let's call it the Golden Noodle. I go in there and right away I'm annoyed. Nobody says hello, nobody offers to take my coat. Then we get put right by the door of the kitchen, people coming and going past our table all the time. When we finally get a chance to order, it turns out that they're out of practically everything on the specials menu.

Host: I'm surprised you didn't walk out.

Chris: I nearly did. I very nearly did. So the food eventually comes. It's overcooked, too salty, a disaster. When the check came, they'd already added the tip!

Host: Right. So what do you want to happen, Chris?

Chris: I want them to stop doing those things!

Host: You won't be eating *there* again, will you?

Chris: Well, of course I will. It's my favorite restaurant!

Unit 11 Self-study

Maria: Hi, Anna. What are you listening to?

Anna: Hi, Maria. It's a podcast about a new course they're having at school. I really like the sound of it.

Maria: Oh, really? What's it in?

Anna: Positive psychology.

Maria: How is it different from normal psychology?

Anna: Listen to the description.

Speaker: While conventional psychology has focused on fear, weakness and **suffering**, positive psychology emphasizes positive values like generosity and **courage**. So, basically, unlike traditional, mainstream psychologists, who try to get rid of anger and **anxiety**, positive psychologists try to help patients build skills that will help them lead a more positive life. Instead of trying to relieve depression, positive psychology tries to build positive emotions, like **gratitude** and **optimism**.

Maria: That sounds really interesting. I sometimes wish I'd majored in psychology. There's so much to learn about.

Anna: You're still interested in literature, though, aren't you?

Maria: Oh, yes. But sometimes I wish I were doing something more, I don't know, more socially important. Sometimes I feel as though I'm a bit **selfish** studying literature.

Anna: Oh, come on! You'll probably use your degree to do something really special. And anyway, positive psychologists say that what they do is focus on the things that make life worth living. And, after all, literature is one of those things that makes life more interesting.

Maria: That's one of the things that's so great about you – you make people feel good about themselves. Positive psychology sounds perfect for you. But I'm not sure you really need a course. What does the course cover?

Anna: The basic science – the research, the various measurement techniques, . . .

Unit 12 Self-study

Trainer: Welcome to the final session of our orientation program. In the general sessions we've discussed issues that will affect all of you, and in the country-specific sessions we have looked at topics like health, climate, language, and the ever popular topic – local cuisine.

Now, all these sessions are important if you are going to enjoy and **benefit** from your time as volunteers. And today's session is central to that goal. We're going to look at culture shock. Now, culture shock is the confusion or anxiety that results when you lose the familiar ways of doing things in everyday situations. Simple things, like not knowing when to shake hands, when and how to accept invitations, and when and how to tip. Although, on *your* monthly allowances, you won't be having to worry too much about tipping.

So, let's look at the first stage of culture shock, sometimes called the honeymoon stage. In this stage you're fascinated by the new and different experiences you're having. It may last for a few days or even a few weeks.

But once you have to seriously **cope** with the stress of being on your own, then the second stage begins: the frustration stage. There are language problems, housing problems, transportation problems, and shopping problems. The local people help you but they don't see why it's such a big deal for you – that's just how things are. So you think they're being insensitive or unsympathetic. They're a bit rude, actually. Cold. Not like people back home. Now here come the stereotypes.

Fortunately, we're going to help you **prepare** for this. And so, once you realize what's going on, you should be ready to move on to the third and final stage: the adjustment stage.

By this time, you will have begun to **succeed** in getting around, in doing things for yourself, and may even be able to **joke** about your difficulties. And after you **adjust** to the differences, you may even begin to enjoy them . . .

Self-study answer key

Unit 1 Self-study
Exercise 1
A
b. Type A personalities are more concerned about goals and deadlines.

B
1. A   3. B
2. B   4. A

C
c. She wants to correct the student without embarrassing him.

Exercise 2
2. flexible   4. content   6. hostile
3. insecure   5. aggressive

Unit 2 Self-study
Exercise 1
A
b. They're very old drawings on the ground.

B
The theories mentioned are:
b. to be alien landing strips
c. to be a guide to the stars
e. to be used in religious ceremonies
f. to be paths between religious sites

C
b. He thinks it's a crazy idea.

Exercise 2
A
1. A   3. A   5. N
2. N   4. N   6. N

B
2. e   4. f   6. b
3. a   5. c

Unit 3 Self-study
Exercise 1
A
c. travel agents

B
1. False   3. False   5. True
2. True   4. True   6. True

C
a. He wants to politely disagree with the person.

Exercise 2
2. f   4. d   6. a
3. e   5. b

Unit 4 Self-study

Exercise 1

A

b. the stages of sleep

B

Stage 1: e	Stage 3: b	Stage 5: d
Stage 2: c	Stage 4: a	

C

b. amused

Exercise 2

A

1. d   2. c   3. b   4. a

B

1. <u>his</u>tory   3. <u>demo</u>nstrate
   <u>histor</u>ian   demon<u>stra</u>tion
   <u>histor</u>ic   de<u>mon</u>strative
   <u>histor</u>ical   de<u>mon</u>strator
   <u>histor</u>ically

2. <u>pho</u>to
   <u>photo</u>graph
   pho<u>tog</u>rapher
   photo<u>graph</u>ic
   pho<u>tog</u>raphy

C

c. The professor was making a joke.

Exercise 2

1. e   3. h   5. g   7. d
2. f   4. b   6. a   8. c

Unit 5 Self-study

Exercise 1

A

a. Different cultures have different communication rules.

B

1. speaking <u>distance</u>
2. speaking <u>volume</u>
3. <u>interruptions</u>

Unit 6 Self-study

Exercise 1

A

c. an island

B

1. True   3. False   5. False
2. False   4. False

C

a. He's interested in it.

Exercise 2

2. f   4. c   6. d   8. g
3. h   5. b   7. e   9. a

Unit 7 Self-study

Exercise 1

A

1. b. visit 50 capital cities in 50 days
2. a. Yes, they did.

B

1. by word of mouth
2. hundreds, if not thousands, of
3. out of their way
4. 116
5. 24,000

C

c. He is expressing his opinion about a subject.

Exercise 2

A

1. il-   4. un-   7. im-
2. dis-   5. dis-   8. ir-
3. dis-   6. im-   9. dis-

B

1. ungrateful   3. illiterate   5. dislike
2. impatient   4. irregular

Unit 8 Self-study

Exercise 1

A

c. clever ideas and inventions

B

The inventions and discoveries the speakers discuss are:

a. polishing shoes with banana peels
c. cleaning a hat with cornmeal
e. the electric guitar

C

a. He thinks it's funny.

Exercise 2

A

1. e   3. a   5. c
2. d   4. b

B

2. noun, verb   4. noun, verb
3. verb, adjective   5. noun, verb

Unit 9 Self-study

Exercise 1

A

b. writing notes for a talk

B

1. village   6. "apartness"
2. 1918   7. 1990
3. lawyer   8. 1993
4. activist   9. 1994
5. 25   10. 1999

C

c. She's asking for information.

Exercise 2

A

2. N   4. N   6. A   8. A
3. N   5. N   7. N

B

2. activist   4. equality
3. famous   5. childhood

Unit 10 Self-study

Exercise 1

A

c. to help people make their complaints more effective

B

1. Be <u>clear</u> in your own <u>mind</u> about <u>why</u> you are dissatisfied.
2. Be <u>clear</u> in your own mind <u>what</u> you want to <u>happen</u> as a <u>result</u> of this complaint.
3. <u>Find</u> <u>out</u> <u>who</u> you should complain to.

C

b. She is fairly certain Chris won't eat there again.

Exercise 2

Somewhat angry: bothered, disgruntled, irritated
Very angry: enraged, furious, livid

Unit 11 Self-study

Exercise 1

A

1. False   2. True   3. False

B

The values and emotions mentioned are:
a. generosity   c. gratitude
b. courage   f. optimism

C

c. Maria thinks Anna is a very positive person.

Exercise 2

1. anxiety   3. selfish   5. optimism
2. suffering   4. courage   6. gratitude

Unit 12 Self-study

Exercise 1

A

1. honeymoon
2. frustration
3. adjustment

B

1. False   3. False
2. True   4. True

C

a. Cultural differences can cause people to misunderstand each other.

Exercise 2

A

1. from   3. for   5. about
2. with   4. in   6. to

B

1. for, to   3. in   5. with, over
2. of   4. on, upon   6. about

Acknowledgments

Illustration credits

Charlene Chua: 8, 80, 81, 97
Paul Daviz: 36
Brad Hamann: 5, 42, 72, 88
Peter Hoey: 17, 64, 70, 96

Larry Jost: 48, 86, 90, 104
Peter McDonnell: 12, 60, 76, 77, 82
Patrick Merewether: 43
Sandy Nichols: 32, 33, 49, 51, 55, 61, 78, 93

Photography credits

2 ©Inmagine; **3** (*left to right*) ©Inmagine; ©DK Stock/Getty Images; ©Inmagine; ©Inmagine; ©Inmagine. **4** (*top to bottom*) ©Inmagine; ©Colin Young-Wolff/Photoedit. **6** (*left to right*) ©The Image Bank/Getty Images; ©Inmagine; ©Inmagine. **7** ©Inmagine. **9** ©Bob Riha, Jr. **10** (*left to right*) ©Inmagine; ©Peter M. Fisher/Corbis; ©Inmagine. **11** ©Stone/Getty Images. **13** ©Inmagine. **14** ©Shutterstock. **15** (*clockwise from top left*) ©Stepfan Rampfel/epa/Corbis; ©Associated Press; ©Bettmann/Corbis. **16** ©Taxi/Getty Images. **18** (*clockwise from top left*) ©Photographer's Choice/Getty Images; ©Stone/Getty Images; ©Inmagine; ©Inmagine. **19** ©GP Bowater/Alamy. **20** ©Shutterstock. **21** (*top to bottom*) ©Bill Bachman/Photoedit; ©Taxi/Getty Images. **22** (*top to bottom*) ©A. Ramey/Photoedit; ©Jeff Greenburg/Photoedit. **24** (*clockwise from top left*) ©Patrick Ward/Corbis; ©Inmagine; ©Shutterstock. **25** (*left to right*) ©Photographer's Choice/Getty Images; ©hemis.fr/Getty Images. **26** ©Inmagine. **27** (*clockwise from top right*) ©Visions of America, LLC/Alamy; ©Danny Lehman/Corbis. **28** (*left to right*) ©Inmagine; ©Inmagine; ©Taxi/Getty Images; ©Inmagine. **29** ©Inmagine. **30** ©Inmagine. **31** ©Inmagine. **35** ©Bill Varie/Corbis. **37** ©Inmagine. **38** ©Inmagine. **39** (*clockwise from top left*) ©Inmagine; ©Inmagine; ©Inmagine. **40** (*clockwise from top left*) ©Riser/Getty Images; ©Inmagine; ©Riser/Getty Images; ©Shutterstock. **44** ©Vince Streano/Corbis. **45** ©Shutterstock. **46** ©Frank Siteman/Photoedit. **47** ©Greg Wahl-Stephens/Associated Press. **50** ©Buzz Pictures/Alamy. **52** ©cjpg/zefa/Corbis. **53** ©Inmagine. **54** ©Inmagine. **56** ©Hugh Threlfall/Alamy. **57** (*top to bottom*) ©Inmagine; ©Bill Aron/Photoedit. **58** (*clockwise from top left*) ©Christine Schneider/zefa/Corbis; ©Inmagine; ©David J. Green – Lifestyle/Alamy; ©David Young-Wolff/Photoedit. **62** (*left to right*) ©Inmagine; ©Inmagine; ©Inmagine; ©Gary Conner/Photoedit. **65** ©David Young-Wolff/Photoedit. **66** (*left to right*) ©Inmagine; ©Inmagine; ©Inmagine. **67** (*left to right*) ©Inmagine; ©Inmagine; ©Photographer's Choice/Getty Images. **68** (*left to right*) ©Dwayne Newton/Photoedit; ©Courtesy of FedEx. **69** ©Yoshikazu Tsuno/Getty Images. **73** ©Simon Marcus/Corbis. **74** ©Helene Rogers/Alamy. **75** (*left to right*) ©Inmagine; ©Inmagine; ©Inmagine. **79** ©Inmagine. **84** (*clockwise from top left*) ©Inmagine; ©Riser/Getty Images; ©Inmagine; ©Photonica/Getty Images; ©Taxi/Getty Images; ©Inmagine. **87** ©Inmagine. **91** ©Inmagine. **92** (*top to bottom*) ©Shutterstock; ©Photographer's Choice/Getty Images; ©Shutterstock; ©Michael Prince/Corbis; ©Shutterstock; ©Shutterstock. **94** ©Inmagine. **95** ©AP Photo/Kristie Bull/Graylock.com. **98** (*clockwise from top left*) ©Inmagine; ©Shutterstock; ©Shutterstock; ©Inmagine. **100** ©Inmagine. **101** (*left to right*) ©Heide Benser/zefa/Corbis; ©Inmagine; ©Photographer's Choice/Getty Images. **102** (*left to right*) ©Inmagine; ©Inmagine; ©Imagestate/Jupiterimages. **103** ©Morgan David de Lossy/Corbis. **105** ©Veer.

Text credits

The authors and publishers are grateful for permission to reprint the following items:

9 Adapted from "Full House: Meet The Silcocks," by Steve Kroft, CBS News Archives. **14** Adapted from "Cartoon-Based Illness Mystifies Japan" Copyright 2007 Reuters. Reprinted with permission from Reuters. Reuters content is the intellectual property of Reuters or its third party content providers. Any copying, republication, or redistribution of Reuters content is expressly prohibited without the prior written consent of Reuters. Reuters shall not be liable for any errors or delays in content, or for any actions taken in reliance thereon. Reuters and the Reuters Sphere Logo are registered trademarks of the Reuters group of companies around the world. For additional information about Reuters content and services, please visit Reuters website at www.reuters.com. Lic # REU-2635-MES. **17** Adapted from "Amnesia Spoils Newlyweds' Bliss" with permission of ABC News. **25** Adapted from "Melbourne and Sydney: A Tale of Two Cities," by Stephen Townsend and Simon Richard. This article was first published in RoughNews, the twice yearly newsletter of Rough Guides publishers, in 1999 © Rough Guides, 80 Strand, London, WC2R 0RL, UK. **43** Adapted from "What Type of Cell Phone User Are You?" by Nancy Friedman, Reprinted with permission of Telephone Doctor Customer Service Training in St. Louis, MO. Nancy Friedman, president, is a keynote speaker at association meetings and Chamber of Commerce events as well as corporate gatherings. Call 314.291.1012 for more information or visit the website at www.telephonedoctor.com. **51** Adapted from "Misadventures in Babysitting," compiled by Martin Cockroft. This article first appeared in the March/April 2000 issue of *Ignite Your Faith*. Used by permission of Christianity Today International, Carol Stream, IL 60188. **61** Adapted from "Brother, Can you Spare a Dime for my Gucci Bills?" by Janelle Brown. This article first appeared in Salon.com, at *http://www.salon.com* An online version remains in the Salon archives. Reprinted with permission. **69** Adapted from "Mr. Song and Dance Man," by Dr. David McNeill, Sophia University, Tokyo. **77** Adapted from "Have you been to the local wailing wall?" Written by Susan Erasmus, www.health24.com. **87** Adapted from "BBC Watchdog Reports: Ave Maria/One Moment in Time." Reprinted with permission. **103** Adapted from "Get Yourself Lost," by Arthur Frommer.

Every effort has been made to trace the owners of copyrighted material in this book. We would be grateful to hear from anyone who recognizes his or her copyrighted material and who is unacknowledged. We will be pleased to make the necessary corrections in future editions of the book.

Answers

Page 44, Exercise 1B: Story 3 is false.